HISTORIC WILMINGTON & THE LOWER CAPE FEAR

An Illustrated History

by Chris E. Fonvielle, Jr.

Commissioned by the Lower Cape Fear Historical Society

Historical Publishing Network
A division of Lammert, Inc.
San Antonio, Texas

Contents

4	PREFACE	
5	CHAPTER I	*The First Cape Fearians*
9	CHAPTER II	*Arrival of the Europeans*
15	CHAPTER III	*Permanent Settlement of the Lower Cape Fear*
23	CHAPTER IV	*The War for Liberty*
31	CHAPTER V	*Antebellum Wilmington*
37	CHAPTER VI	*Wilmington Turned "Topsy-Turvy" by Civil War*
45	CHAPTER VII	*The African American Experience*
53	CHAPTER VIII	*The Greatest Generation of Cape Fearians*
59	CHAPTER IX	*Wilmington Yesterday and Today*
64	APPENDIX	
68	BIBLIOGRAPHY	
69	SHARING THE HERITAGE	

First Edition

Copyright © 2007 Historical Publishing Network

All rights reserved. No part of this book may be reproduced in any form or by any means, electronic or mechanical, including photocopying, without permission in writing from the publisher. All inquiries should be addressed to Historical Publishing Network, 11555 Galm Road, Suite 100, San Antonio, Texas, 78254. Phone (800) 749-9790.

ISBN: 978-1-893619-68-5
Library of Congress Card Catalog Number: 2007921599

Historic Lower Cape Fear: An Illustrated History

author:	Chris E. Fonvielle, Jr.
photo researcher:	Eric Dabney
cover artist:	Mary Ellen Golden
contributing writer for "Sharing the Heritage":	Joe Goodpasture

Historical Publishing Network

president:	Ron Lammert
project managers:	Carol Egan, Roger Smith
director of operations:	Charles A. Newton, III
administration:	Angela Lake, Donna M. Mata, Judi Free, Diane Perez
book sales:	Dee Steidle
production:	Colin Hart, Craig Mitchell, Michael Reaves, Evelyn Hart

PRINTED IN SINGAPORE

Dedication

The Lower Cape Fear Historical Society was chartered in 1956 to "collect and preserve historical records, artifacts and materials and disseminate knowledge and information pertaining to the history of the Lower Cape Fear area."

The Society is proud to celebrate fifty years of being an integral part of this community. Members of the Historical Society began plans to make Fort Fisher a state historic site, helped create the Historic Wilmington Foundation for preservation purposes, started historic walking and house tours, erected historic markers and published significant and unique historical works in book and pamphlet form. Informational programs throughout the fifty years have addressed topical issues in the community through speakers and presentations. Specialized programs for students enhance the school curricula. The Lower Cape Fear Historical Society is based in the Latimer House, an 1852 mansion with elegant Victorian furnishings and gardens, which is one of Wilmington's three historic-tour homes.

We hope you will enjoy this book, whether you are a Wilmington native or a recently arrived resident. It gives us all the opportunity to learn more about our historic area. We are proud to present it as it continues the celebration of the rich history of this area and the fascinating story of the varied people who have made it their home.

Candace McGreevy
Executive Director

Author's Dedication

In Memory of Chris E. Fonvielle (1921-1970) and Daniel D. Cameron (1921-2005)
— best of friends, then and now.

PREFACE

I love pictorial history books! I remember receiving my first one, *The Golden Book of the Civil War* by the editors of *American Heritage*, as a Christmas gift from my parents, Gene and Jane Fonvielle, in 1961. It was the first year of the Civil War Centennial and I was eight years old. I spent hours and hours perusing the period photographs, lithographs, and engravings, imagining what that terrible war must have been like. Forty-six years later I still treasure the book that now enjoys a prominent place on my library bookshelf. Imagine my excitement then at being asked by the Lower Cape Fear Historical Society to do an illustrated history of Wilmington and the Lower Cape Fear, where I was born and raised.

As the book title indicates, this work is an illustrated history of the region's past. It is not a comprehensive study. Lammert Incorporated contracted me to select approximately 125 images depicting people, places, and life in and around the Wilmington area and to provide an accompanying brief narrative. I decided to focus on the region's earlier history as it most interested me and had been less covered in previous similar works, including Anne Russell's *Wilmington: A Pictorial History* (Norfolk, 1981), Diane Cobb Cashman's *Cape Fear Adventure: An Illustrated History of Wilmington* (Wilmington, 1982), Robert M. Fales's *Wilmington Yesteryear* (Wilmington, 1984), Susan Taylor Block's *Along the Cape Fear* (Charleston, 1998) and *Cape Fear Lost* (Charleston, 1999) and Ann Hewlett Hutteman's *Wilmington, North Carolina* (Charleston, 2000). Andrew Koeppel's *Wilmington Then and Now* (Wilmington, 1999) and Beverly Tetterton's *Wilmington: Lost But Not Forgotten* (Wilmington, 2005) examine the city's historic residences, public buildings and preservation movement. These pictorial histories are all fine works in their own right and I greatly admire and respect the authors.

I purposely chose not to emphasize the history of Wilmington and the Lower Cape Fear during the late nineteenth and twentieth centuries as together the published pictorial histories have covered them well. I did not, however, completely neglect these time periods. Indeed, Wilmington played a crucial role during World War II, about which Wilbur D. Jones, Jr. wrote in *Sentimental Journey: Memoirs of a Wartime Boomtown* (Shippensburg, 2002) and *The Journey Continues: The World War II Home Front* (Shippensburg, 2005).

Wilmington has never been more important in our country's past than during wartime. *Historic Wilmington & The Lower Cape Fear: An Illustrated History* therefore looks closely at the Revolutionary War, the Civil War, and World War II in the region. The Revolution was fought for independence and liberty. The colony's most ardent defenders of liberty resided in the Lower Cape Fear. The Civil War was fought over the meaning of the Union and freedom. Wilmington emerged as the Confederacy's principal seaport by 1863 and its most important city by late the following year. World War II was fought to rid the world of totalitarianism. The Lower Cape Fear sent thousands of soldiers and hundreds of locally manufactured ships to assist Allied victory in both Europe and the Pacific.

For the most part, the narrative herein unfolds chronologically. In addition to the region's history during the three major American wars, I look at the less well known story of the Lower Cape Fear's earliest human inhabitants, the arrival of the Europeans in the area, settlement, development, and expansion, and Cape Fear life in the late twentieth century. I also focus on the African-American experience and Cape Fear sports, recreation, and entertainment.

The book's cover and title page bear my name but the project was truly a joint effort. I extend my heartfelt appreciation to the following people and institutions for their assistance, guidance, and encouragement: Eric Dabney; LuAnn Mims and Candace McGreevy, Lower Cape Fear Historical Society; Ron Lammert of Lammert Publications, Inc.; Beverly Tetterton, Joseph Sheppard, and Adam Berenbak, New Hanover County Public Library; Sue Miller, Cape Fear Museum; Richard Lawrence, Underwater Archaeology Unit, Fort Fisher, North Carolina; Steve McAllister, McAllister & Solomon Used and Rare Books; Peter Friztler, Larry Usilton, David LaVere, Adina Riggins, Gerald Parnell, and Joe Browning, UNC Wilmington; Ryan Pierce, Wrightsville Beach Museum; Jim McKee, Madeline "Punk" Spencer, Mary Strickland, and Deb Worden, Southport Maritime Museum; Wilbur D. Jones, Jr.; David Norris; Melva Calder; Nancy Beeler; Charles V. Peery; Anna Pennington; Jim Pleasants; Everard Smith; Joe Funderburg; Janet Seapker; David Stallman; R. Vollers Hanson; Sherry Niven; Martin Peebles; Peter Tuite; William B. Gould IV; and Mary Ann Powell. Many thanks also to my colleague Dr. Alan D. Watson, Department of History, UNC Wilmington, for reading and editing much of the manuscript. The same goes for my wife Nancy, who offered constructive criticism, helpful suggestions, and a lot of patience as I worked to complete the project. Read, peruse, and enjoy!

Chris E. Fonvielle, Jr.
Department of History, University of North Carolina Wilmington

Cape Fear Indian projectile points and pottery shards found by the author in and around the Wilmington area, including his own backyard on Greenville Sound.
COURTESY OF MELVA CALDER PHOTOGRAPHY.

Chapter I

The First Cape Fearians

The arrow narrowly missed its human target, the stone-tipped projectile burying itself instead deep into the upper edge of the small boat. Startled by the surprise attack, William Hilton and his fellow English explorers quickly turned their heads to see who was shooting at them, catching a glimpse of a lone bowman on a steep bluff high above the Cape Fear River. They immediately recognized him as one in a group of four seemingly friendly Indians from whom they had purchased a basket of acorns only a short time before. Angered by a sense of betrayal, Hilton and his crew stormed ashore, hoping to capture and punish the attacker. By the time they reached his perch, however, the Indian had fled, escaping into the forest.

As the Englishmen proceeded on their journey down the Cape Fear River, they came upon a canoe beached along the shoreline, which they presumed belonged to their antagonist. They went ashore to destroy the vessel, and in the process discovered his hut, which they tore down in a fit of anger. They also smashed his personal belongings and took a basket of acorns before returning to the safety of their ship, the *Adventure*, anchored further downriver.

Neither Hilton nor history reveals the name or the motive of the defiant Indian, although Hilton recounted the ambush in his journal entry of November 23, 1663, naming the site where it occurred Mount Skerry. It is unlikely that historians will ever learn his identity and can only speculate as to why he ambushed the Englishmen. Perhaps he was merely dissatisfied with the transaction for the acorns and sought revenge. Or maybe his motive was more complex. Perhaps he feared that the white men posed a serious threat to his people and his world, and hoped that a show of force would drive them away and dissuade them, or others like them, from ever returning to this land.

Whatever his intention, however, his errant bowshot was symbolic of things to come.

Historians know little about the Native Americans who roamed the Lower Cape Fear before being swept away by the advancing tide of European civilization. Although they resided in the area for about ten thousand years before white people arrived, the Indians had no written language to leave behind accounts of their lives, their deeds, or their stories. Archaeologists have discovered only one site, as yet unexcavated, that may contain a late Woodland period village, A.D. 500-1000, and comparatively few artifacts that would reveal more about the culture and society of the Cape Fear's first human inhabitants. What modern day researchers know about the Indians comes primarily from European reports of encounters with them before they had largely disappeared by the eighteenth century.

The earliest recorded observation of the Cape Fear Indians and their land came from the pen of Giovanni da Verrazzano, the "gentleman explorer" from Tuscany, who, as a contract sailor in the employ of King Francis I of France, searched the Atlantic coastline for a water passageway to Asia. On March 1, 1524, Verrazzano's ship, *La Dauphine*, made landfall at 34° latitude, which would have put him slightly above Cape Fear in the area of present-day Myrtle Grove Sound. Verrazzano missed the entrance to the river and, in fact, made no mention of its existence in his journal.

Exploring northward along the shore, Verrazzano and his crewmen encountered native people, whom they found to be friendly and curious, if somewhat skittish. Verrazzano described them as "dark in color, not unlike Ethiopians, with thick black haire, not very long, tied back behind their head like a small tail. As for the physique of these men, they are well proportioned, of medium height, a little taller than we are. They have broad chests, strong arms, and their legs and other parts of the body are well composed." Verrazzano's impressions of the Cape Fear Indians' physical characteristics compared favorably with John White's watercolors of Secotan Indians he met and painted in North Carolina's northern coastal plain some years later. "We could not learn the details of the life and customs of these people," Verrazzano lamented, "because of the short time we spent on land, due to the fact that there were few men, and the ship was anchored on the high seas."

Perhaps the Indians William Hilton encountered during his three expeditions to the Lower Cape Fear, 1662-1663, were descendants of those Verrazzano had met more than a century earlier. On his first exploratory mission to the region in October 1662, Hilton described them as "very poor and silly [simple] Creatures…they are not numerous, for in all our various travels for three weeks and more, we saw not 100 in all, they were very courteous to us, and afraid of us, but They are very theevish." On his third trip to the Cape Fear the following autumn, Hilton found the local Indians to be greater in number than he had initially believed, but still friendly. Hilton's opinion of them lessened, however, after one of them ambushed

❖
Above: Verrazzano's description of the Cape Fear Indians compared favorably with John White's watercolors of Secotan Indians, including this warrior, in northeastern North Carolina about 1585.
COURTESY OF THE BRITISH MUSEUM, LONDON.

Top, right: North Carolina Indian village about 1585.
COURTESY OF THE BRITISH MUSEUM, LONDON.

Right English explorer William Hilton and his crew were fired upon by a Cape Fear Indian with whom they had recently struck a deal for a basket of acorns as they journeyed by boat down the Cape Fear River in the autumn of 1663.
COURTESY OF THE BRITISH MUSEUM, LONDON.

him and his crew at Mount Skerry, the location of which has yet to be determined.

Unfortunately, scant European reports and archaeological evidence sheds little light on the Indians who lived in the Lower Cape Fear far longer than either Europeans or Americans. Nonetheless, anthropologists and ethnohistorians have come to some plausible conclusions about them, believing, for example, that they were members of the Eastern Sioux language group. At the time of European contact with Native Americans, there were three major language groups—Siouan, Algonquian, and Iroquian—and more than thirty nations or groups in what would become North Carolina. The Cape Fears, as they are commonly called, appear to have been one of the smaller Siouxan nations, probably numbering in the hundreds, assuming European reports are accurate. In fact, they may not have been a distinctive group at all, but were perhaps members of the Waccamaws that resided around Lake Waccamaw, west of the Cape Fear. Rivers and lakes often assumed the name of the people that lived within close proximity of them—Waccamaw, Roanoke, Chowan, Neuse, Pee Dee, and Pasquotank, for example—but that was not the case for the Cape Fear Indians.

Historians do not know the name by which the Cape Fears called themselves. Indeed, they are the only Carolina Indian group that goes by the name Europeans, presumably William Hilton, bestowed upon them. Some historians suggest that the name of the Cape Fears, or that of the river, may have been Saponi, as one old map shows that name in the upper Cape Fear River valley. Scholars continue to uncover tidbits of information that enhance their understanding of them. Two recently discovered colonial documents in South Carolina have led Blair A. Rudes, a professor of ethnohistory at the University of North Carolina Charlotte, to speculate that the Cape Fears knew themselves as Daw-Hees.

Whatever their origins and whatever their name, the native people of the Lower Cape Fear were primitive, at least as far as the Europeans were concerned. They lived a semi-nomadic life, traveling from the country to the coast to exploit abundant marine resources. They combined fishing and the harvesting of shellfish with hunting and gathering. The surrounding woods and fields were abundant with whitetail deer, black bear, small game, and turkeys, as well as acorns, pecans, and scuppernong grapes. To supplement their diets, they planted corn and beans in communal fields and small family plots that the men cleared from the forests and women tended. Hilton and his men described the Indians' corn stalks as being 11 or 12 feet tall, higher than any they had seen before. Cattle and hogs, which the Cape Fears inherited from European settlers, later became an important Indian food as well.

Leadership among the Cape Fears, as with most Carolina Indian groups, rested in the

✧

Above: The Cape Fear Indians exploited abundant marine resources along the Carolina coast for sustenance.
COURTESY OF THE BRITISH MUSEUM, LONDON.

Below: Giovanni da Verrazzano reportedly was the first European to encounter the Native Americans of the Lower Cape Fear when he made landfall in the region in early March 1524.
COURTESY OF THE NORTH CAROLINA STATE ARCHIVES.

hands of a male chief, called "king" by the English, and his advisers. Hilton purchased the river and adjacent land from Wattcoosa and "such other Indians as appeared to us to be chief of those parts."

Wattcoosa and his people lived in small towns or villages. One town was called Necoes, a place that Hilton visited, although he referred to it as an "Indian plantation." Suggesting that a village was located along what is today Town Creek in Brunswick County on the west side of the Cape Fear River, Hilton named the waterway "Indian River." Reportedly there were five Indian towns in the Lower Cape Fear in 1715.

The absence of archaeological evidence only bolsters the argument that the Cape Fear Indians were few in number and relatively weak militarily. Unable to defend themselves against whites and stronger Indian rivals, they eventually either left the area or turned to the English for protection becoming, in essence, "tributary Indians." One price they paid for English security was a military alliance against the Tuscaroras in a war that raged along the Neuse and Pamlico rivers in North Carolina, 1711-1713. The Cape Fears and Yamasees joined forces with South Carolina militia commanded first by Colonel John Barnwell and then, beginning in March 1712, by Colonel James Moore and his brother Captain Maurice Moore. By the following year, the Tuscaroras were crushed by the Moore-led coalition army, and most of them driven from the area. Maurice Moore remained to live in North Carolina at war's end.

When Yamasee Indians attacked white settlers along the South Carolina frontier beginning in 1715, Maurice Moore took a force of militiamen and loyal Tuscarora and Coree warriors down the coast to assist his former colony. Their line of march led them through the Lower Cape Fear. En route, Moore learned of an alleged plot by dissident Cape Fears and Waccamaws to ambush his force. Armed with that intelligence, he avoided the trap and instead struck unmercifully against the Cape Fears and crushed them. The battle may have occurred at Sugar Loaf hill on the east side of the Cape Fear River in the present day Carolina Beach State Park. The Cape Fears disappeared in the wake of their defeat at the hands of Maurice Moore and his army. Hugh Meredith, a visitor to the region in 1730, observed that not a single Indian was to be found, they having been killed off by the English and other foes, with only a few survivors reportedly living in fear and squalor at Winyah Bay, South Carolina.

If the defiant Cape Fear Indian who ambushed William Hilton and his sailors in 1663 had done so out of concern for the future of his people and their culture, his fears proved prophetic. Only fifty-two years after he let that arrow fly toward his English targets, the Cape Fears were gone from the land.

✧
Local lore has it that this ancient, gnarled oak known as "The Indian Tree" pointed the way to fishing grounds for Native Americans near present-day Southport.
COURTESY OF ERIC DABNEY.

Chapter II

Arrival of the Europeans

Giovanni da Verrazzano, sailing for France, left the earliest extant European account of the Cape Fear region and its native inhabitants in 1524, although Spanish from the West Indies and accompanying missionary priests may have sailed in the area before then as they explored the Atlantic seaboard. In 1521, Francisco Gordillo led a Spanish party that examined the south Atlantic coast. Five years later Lucas Vasquez de Ayllon, a Spanish lawyer and bureaucrat of Hispaniola, attempted to settle the mainland with an expedition of five hundred men, women, and African slaves. The settlement, San Miguel de Gualdape, collapsed within a few months, however, doomed by bad weather, disease, and the death of its leader. For decades historians and archaeologists speculated that San Miguel had been located on the banks of the Cape Fear River. To date, however, archaeologists have discovered no remains of the town or concentration of Spanish artifacts in the region, leading most historians to now believe that the settlement was probably in South Carolina or Georgia.

The failure of San Miguel de Gualdape discouraged Spain from further serious attempts to colonize the upper Atlantic coast, but emboldened other European nations to challenge Spain's claim to the New World. In 1562, French explorers made a futile attempt to settle at Port Royal in what is now South Carolina, but was then claimed by Spain as a part of Florida. More than twenty years later Sir Walter Ralegh (the more accepted spelling of his surname at the time) dispatched two English expeditions to settle Virginia at Roanoke Island, with the last one mysteriously disappearing after 1587. While Ralegh's failures dampened enthusiasm for colonization for twenty years, the English finally established a foothold in America at Jamestown in 1607. English colonization of America proceeded in fits and starts after that, interrupted by civil war in the 1640s, the beheading of King Charles I, eleven years of contentious rule by Oliver Cromwell and the Roundheads, and finally, Restoration of the Stuart House under King Charles II in 1660.

To show his gratitude to eight powerful men who had remained loyal to the Crown during its troubles, Charles II granted them land in Virginia. On March 24, 1663, the king conveyed to the

❖

Led by John Vassal, the "Adventurers and Planters of Cape Feare" from Barbados founded Charles Towne in late May 1664, on this site at the mouth of what is today Town Creek in Brunswick County.

COURTESY OF CHRIS E. FONVIELLE, JR.

Lords Proprietors a vast tract located between 31° and 36° latitude, which included the Cape Fear, to be called Carolina (Latin for Charles). By then, however, Englishmen and women were already living in the Lower Cape Fear.

In early October 1662, William Hilton of Charlestowne, Massachusetts Bay, had arrived at the Cape Fear, looking for a suitable spot to settle a small group of Puritans. How Hilton came to learn of the Cape Fear or discovered the river, apparently the first European to do so, is unclear. At any rate, Hilton, on board the *Adventure*, spent more than three weeks exploring the waterway, which he named the Charles River, and its tributaries. He mistakenly believed that the northeast branch was the river's main arm. The reconnaissance led Hilton to form a favorable impression of the region's climate and land, with its great forests, fields, and abundant wild game and fowl. Although less affected by the Indians he and his men encountered, Hilton believed they were too few in number to pose a threat to settlement.

Hilton's glowing report of his discoveries encouraged the rapid organization of a group of colonists who called themselves the Adventurers About Cape Fayre. They soon arrived in the Lower Cape Fear, probably in February 1663, but remained less than two months. Where the New Englanders established their beachhead and what happened to discourage them is not known. They may have resented being so far away from family and friends, encountered hostile Indians, or simply not liked the area. Whatever caused their dissatisfaction, the Puritans beat a hasty retreat. In doing so, they abandoned their livestock on present-day Bald Head Island at the mouth of the river and erected a signpost with a note attached, cautioning other would-be settlers that the Cape Fear was an inhospitable place to be avoided.

After transporting members of the ill-fated expedition back to Massachusetts Bay, Hilton sailed southward to the thriving English colony of Barbados in the Lesser Antilles. There he found interest in his colonization proposal from John Vassall, who contracted with Hilton to make a second voyage of discovery to determine the most advantageous place to establish a settlement along the Atlantic seaboard. Still on board the *Adventure*, Hilton departed Barbados in August 1663 and sailed up the coast. Already familiar with the Charles River area, Hilton again concentrated his efforts there. On October 16, 1663, he and his crew entered the waterway which they renamed the Cape Fayre River, perhaps to sever all association with the earlier settlement debacle. The Englishmen spent the following seven weeks exploring the area, especially the northeast river, and named several landmarks such as Rocky Point, Stag Park, and Turkey Quarters. Hilton and his men also traveled up the northwest branch where they observed good high ground and well timbered forests and

✧

The Tuscan "gentleman explorer" Giovanni da Verrazzano and his crew were sailing for France when they made the first documented visit by Europeans to the Lower Cape Fear in the late winter of 1524.
COURTESY OF THE LOWER CAPE FEAR HISTORICAL SOCIETY.

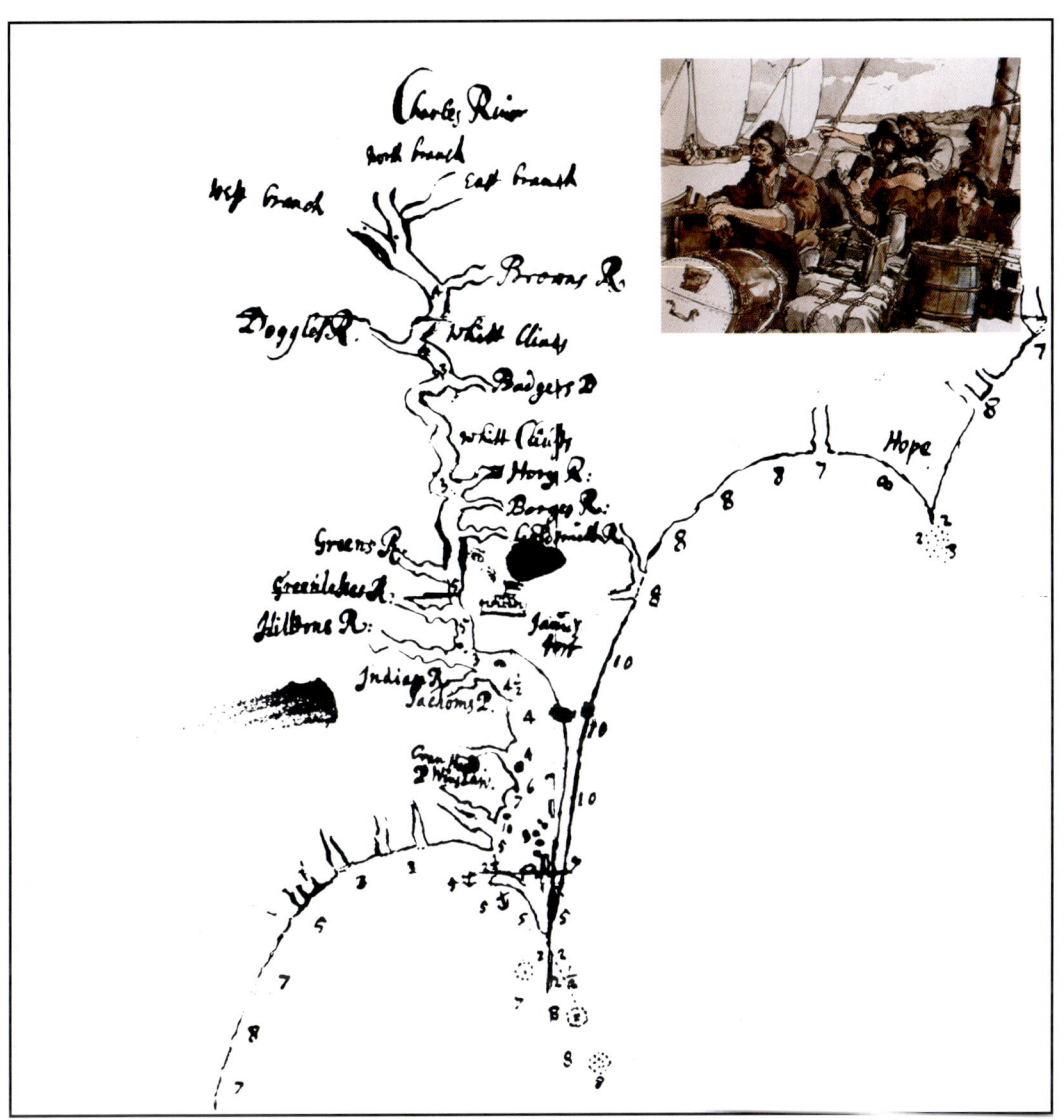

Earliest English map of the Lower Cape Fear drawn by Nicholas Shapley in 1662.
COURTESY OF THE LOWER CAPE FEAR HISTORICAL SOCIETY.

traded with a group of Indians, one of whom later ambushed them with bow and arrow. Even so, Hilton was determined to colonize the Cape Fear, which he demonstrated by purchasing the river and adjacent lands from King Wattcoosa and other local leaders.

Hilton departed the Cape Fear in early December 1663 and returned to Barbados by the following month. Intrigued by Hilton's optimistic report and land acquisition, John Vassall made arrangements to colonize the Cape Fear with a party calling itself "the Adventurers and Planters of Cape Feare" (Cape Fayre, Cape Feare, and Cape Fear were used interchangeably in the days of exploration). Overcrowding and exorbitant land prices in Barbados compelled many subsistence farmers to look elsewhere for a place to live and Carolina attracted them in large part because land was abundant and uninhabited by Europeans.

While agents for the Adventurers negotiated terms of settlement with the Lords Proprietors in London, John Vassall, perhaps accompanied by William Hilton, led the first settlers to the Cape Fear, where they landed on May 29, 1664. They constructed a fortification and trading center on the north bank of Indian River (its location at the mouth of present-day Town Creek confirmed by archaeologists), about twenty miles above the river's entranceway. According to a propaganda pamphlet designed to entice additional colonists to Charles Towne, as the settlement was named, private homes and farms were soon scattered sixty miles up and down the river and adjoining streams. Their specific locations, however, are a mystery as archaeologists have yet to discover the remains of even a single seventeenth century house in the area.

CHAPTER II

By 1665, Charles Towne had been incorporated into a county called Clarendon, named for Edward Hyde, earl of Clarendon and one of the Lords Proprietors. Despite its recognition and hopeful beginning, however, the colony soon faltered, a victim of circumstances, indifference, and neglect. Farmers unfortunate enough to have been allotted land on the east side of the Cape Fear River were dissatisfied with the white sandy soil among the pine barrens that was largely unsuitable for growing crops. Land on the west side of the river tended to be higher, black and fertile or good lowland marshes for rice fields. Other colonists shied away from the area for fear of acquiring bad land. Moreover, arbitrators never reached satisfactory terms of settlement with the Lords Proprietors, who expressed more interest in a proposed colony further to the south.

Sir John Yeamans, a royalist émigré and prominent planter in Barbados, used his influence with the Lords Proprietors to undermine Charles Towne on the Cape Fear in favor of his planned settlement in South Carolina. Even after visiting Charles Towne in late 1665, Yeamans took little interest in its well-being or that of its colonists. The same was true of the Lords Proprietors, preoccupied as they and the government were with the plague that decimated England, 1664-1666; the Great Fire of London in the summer of 1666; and the Dutch War, 1665-1667. To make matters worse, evidence suggests that the tenuous peaceful co-existence between the Charles Towne settlers and the Cape Fear Indians deteriorated into violence.

Despite John Vassall's best efforts to keep the colony alive, an increasing number of unhappy settlers abandoned Charles Towne. By the autumn of 1667 the settlement was deserted, its farms and houses falling into disrepair, and its former residents removed to Albemarle County, North Carolina, or Virginia. The first English attempts to inhabit the Lower Cape Fear had ended in failure.

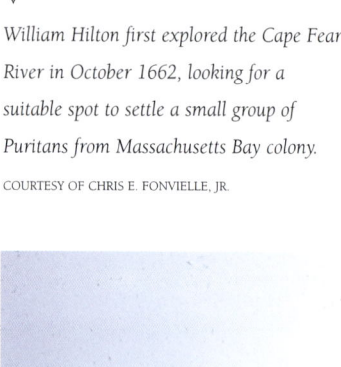

William Hilton first explored the Cape Fear River in October 1662, looking for a suitable spot to settle a small group of Puritans from Massachusetts Bay colony.
COURTESY OF CHRIS E. FONVIELLE, JR.

Unless a few brave souls remained behind to live among the ruins of Charles Towne or shipwreck survivors managed to tough it out in the Cape Fear wilderness, of which there are no records, Europeans did not inhabit the region again for another fifty-eight years. Perhaps there was hope among the Cape Fear Indians that white people might never return. To dissuade them from doing so, the Cape Fears allegedly killed sailors stranded on the coast by storms and shipwrecks.

In 1670, English settlers established a new Charles Towne (now Charleston) in South Carolina that John Yeamans had planned to settle a few years before. The towns of Bath, New Bern, and Edenton in Albemarle County, North Carolina, also emerged before colonists again attempted to people the Cape Fear. Sparsely populated as the Carolina coast was in the early eighteenth century, it soon became a haven for pirates who prowled the shipping lanes for unsuspecting prey and hid behind barrier islands.

The Cape Fear estuary, with its shoal waters and sandy islands, was an ideal spot for pirates to hide. Local legends abound of buccaneers roaming Bald Head Island and Captain William Kidd burying a chest of gold on Money Island at Wrightsville Sound. Spanish coins from the early 1700s were reportedly found on Bald Head and people dug on Money Island for more than one hundred years searching for Captain Kidd's elusive treasure, but history reveals only one real pirate episode at the Cape Fear.

Stede Bonnet, the "gentleman pirate" from Barbados, met his fate in the Cape Fear estuary. The former English army officer was a man of considerable wealth and refinement when he turned to pirating, allegedly to escape boredom or a nagging wife. After

Above: By 1665, Charles Towne along the Cape Fear River had been incorporated into a county called Clarendon, named for Edward Hyde, earl of Clarendon and one of the Lords Proprietors.
COURTESY OF THE NORTH CAROLINA STATE ARCHIVES.

Below: Charles Towne settlers unfortunate enough to have been allotted land on the sandy east side of the Cape Fear River soon grew dissatisfied and departed the colony, contributing to its break up.
COURTESY OF CHRIS E. FONVIELLE, JR.

CHAPTER II

❖

Above: For more than one hundred years Cape Fear residents dug for pirate treasure allegedly buried by Captain William Kidd on Money Island across from the mouth of Bradley Creek at Wrightsville Sound. Unfortunately, Money Island, seen here in the early twentieth century, is now covered with spoil dredged from the Intracoastal Waterway by the U.S. Corps of Engineers.
COURTESY OF THE LOWER CAPE FEAR HISTORICAL SOCIETY.

Below: The "gentleman pirate" Stede Bonnet was taken captive by Colonel William Rhett of South Carolina after a fierce naval battle in the Cape Fear estuary on September 27, 1718.
COURTESY OF THE LOWER CAPE FEAR HISTORICAL SOCIETY.

preying along the Virginia and Carolina coasts in his ten-gun sloop *Revenge*, Bonnet joined forces with the infamous Edward Teach, better known as "Blackbeard." Together they terrorized Charleston, South Carolina, in May 1718, capturing ships, taking hostages, and demanding ransom. From Charleston, Blackbeard and Bonnet sailed up the coast to North Carolina, ostensibly to take an oath to the king and relinquish pirating. While Bonnet and his crew surrendered to Governor Charles Eden, however, Blackbeard betrayed them and, in true pirate style, took off with all the booty.

An enraged Bonnet pursued Blackbeard, but was unable to catch his unsavory former associate. Disenchanted, Bonnet renounced his oath and resumed piracy. He stalked the North Carolina coast, taking prizes and plunder during the summer of 1718. On August 12 of that year, Bonnet in his renamed ship the *Royal James*, and with two prize vessels, crossed the Cape Fear bar to careen, reorganize, and rest. There Bonnet dawdled too long, which led to his downfall.

The South Carolina government, incensed by Blackbeard and Bonnet's campaign of terror against Charleston, authorized Colonel William Rhett to bring the pirates to justice. With two-ships, Rhett sailed northward in mid-September 1718, only to discover Bonnet's hideout at the Cape Fear. Bonnet tried to make his getaway in the *Royal James*, but Rhett chased the pirate aground in shallow water and forced him to surrender after a fierce battle. The naval showdown allegedly occurred at the mouth of Bonnet's Creek near present-day Southport in Brunswick County. Wherever the engagement took place, the golden age of piracy in the Lower Cape Fear apparently began and ended with the capture of Bonnet and his crew. Rhett returned with his prisoners to Charleston, where they were promptly tried, convicted, and executed. Justice was swift as Bonnet swung from the gallows on December 10, 1718.

With the passing of the Cape Fear Indians and the removal of pirates from the Cape Fear, the area was now open to European settlement.

Chapter III

Permanent Settlement of the Lower Cape Fear

Historians generally consider Maurice Moore from South Carolina to be the father of permanent settlement in the Lower Cape Fear, but George Burrington should share that claim to fame. Burrington envisioned great things for the region when he became the proprietary governor of North Carolina in 1724. The good land would attract settlers, wood products from the vast forests could be used in building fleets of English ships, and the Cape Fear River and its tributaries would serve as the lifeblood of a viable commercial trade. Burrington reasoned that he might also personally benefit from the development, but he faced a dilemma.

The Cape Fear was contested territory, a sort of no man's land between South Carolina and North Carolina. The two immense counties had once been part of the same proprietary, but had since separated economically and politically. While South Carolina's economy flourished in rice and slaves, North Carolina struggled in comparative poverty and political factionalism. The Cape Fear River became the unofficial boundary between the two counties, and the Lords Proprietors prohibited land ownership in the area to prevent land speculation and corruption. The only proprietary land grant in the Cape Fear was Bald Head Island, awarded to Landgrave Thomas Smith of South Carolina on May 8, 1713.

George Burrington's answer to the proprietary ban on land distribution in the Lower Cape Fear was simply to ignore it. If things went his way, the Cape Fear might even become an independent province and satisfy his own ambition and interests. To encourage settlement, the newly appointed governor surveyed the river and inspected its adjoining lands in the winter of 1724-1725. Then, in the spring of 1725, Burrington, without permission from the Lords Proprietors, began issuing land warrants that would allow colonists to occupy property until such time as terms of settlement could be realized or rejected.

✧

Brunswick Town was built on low bluffs along the west side of the Cape Fear River twelve miles from its mouth. Remains of the colonial ghost town can still be seen at what is today the Brunswick Town-Fort Anderson State Historic Site.

COURTESY OF CHRIS E. FONVIELLE, JR.

Maurice Moore, who came from a wealthy and influential family in the Goose Creek section of Berkeley County near Charleston, South Carolina, was the first recipient of Burrington's controversial land allocation program. Moore was already familiar with the Lower Cape Fear, having traveled through it during the Yamasee War and having struck the final blow against the Cape Fear Indians in 1715. He initially acquired more than seven thousand acres of land from Burrington and was appointed to the governor's council. Maurice's younger brother Roger also received property that would become the core of Orton Plantation.

❖

St. Philip's Anglican Church, its massive brick walls built to withstand the strongest hurricanes, is the only standing colonial structure at Brunswick Town.

COURTESY OF CHRIS E. FONVIELLE, JR.

Maurice Moore was the earliest known permanent English resident of the Lower Cape Fear, establishing himself in the region by the end of April 1726. One of the first places he built a house was the former site of Charles Towne, the ruins of which apparently could still be seen, as he named the property Old Town Plantation. The nearby stream subsequently became known as Old Town Creek or simply Town Creek. Maurice's brothers Roger, Nathaniel, and John and sisters Mary and Rebecca followed him to the Lower Cape Fear, as did a host of other family members and friends from South Carolina—Eleazer Allen, William Dry, Nathaniel Rice, and Richard Eagles. They left their home province to take advantage of Burrington's liberal land distribution policy at the Cape Fear, but also to escape high taxes and maladministration by the South Carolina government. Relatives of Maurice by marriage also soon arrived from Albemarle County, North Carolina, including his brother-in-law Edward Moseley along with members of the influential Swann, Ashe, and Harnett families. So strong were the connections and power of the Moores and their supporters that together they became known throughout the Lower Cape Fear as "the Family."

In keeping with Burrington's dream of the Cape Fear becoming a place of brisk trade and commerce, Maurice and Roger Moore donated 360 acres of land for a port town. Clearly the Moores hoped to curry favor with the reigning British monarch, George I, who was a member of the German House of Brunswick, Hanover, when they named their town Brunswick. It was located about twelve miles from the mouth of the river on low bluffs on the west side of the Cape Fear River at a point deep enough to accommodate large ocean-going vessels.

The Moores intended for Brunswick to become a place of considerable importance, but settlement was slow going. While the Lords Proprietors turned a blind eye to their appointed governor's land scheme in the Cape Fear, they also took little interest in Brunswick's development as it occurred simultaneously with the end of proprietary rule and the beginning of royal government in Carolina in 1729. The Crown, however, made Brunswick the seat of economic, political, and ecclesiastical authority in New Hanover Precinct at the time of royal rule. Brunswick County was carved out of New Hanover in 1764.

By 1731, Port Brunswick had become Great Britain's main port of entry in the southern area of North Carolina, with all ships entering and exiting the harbor required to clear there. Brunswick was also the home of the colony's executive branch of government for a time. The governor's council met in Brunswick, although the General Assembly never did, and two royal governors—Arthur Dobbs and his successor William Tryon—lived at nearby Russellborough. When Arthur

Dobbs died in 1765 after eleven years of rule, his remains were buried inside St. Philip's Anglican Church at Brunswick, the first church in the parish. Today the massive brick walls of St. Philip's, built 1754-1768, are the only standing remains of a colonial structure in the ghost town of Brunswick.

Many members of "the Family" resided in Brunswick and it remained the most important port on the Cape Fear River until the American Revolution, but it never really amounted to much of a town. Described by one visitor as "an inconsiderable place," no more than 250 residents ever lived there, half of them being mostly merchants, mariners, planters, and artisans and their and wives and children and the other half being black slaves. Janet Schaw, the Scottish author of *Journal of a Lady of Quality* who resided at Brunswick for a brief time in 1775, observed that "tho' the best sea port in the province, the town is very poor—a few scattered houses on the edge of the woods, without street or regularity." Brunswick seemingly faced persistent problems throughout its existence reflecting the weakness and vulnerability of the settlement on the Cape Fear River decades after it was founded.

In 1748, the final year of King George's War between England and the alliance of Spain and France, Spanish naval forces attacked Brunswick. In early September, the Spanish sloops *Fortuna* and *Loretta* crossed the Cape Fear bar, ostensibly to kidnap slaves working on Fort Johnston, then under construction near the mouth of the harbor. As it was a Sunday, army engineers had halted work on the fort and taken the slaves to Brunswick to rest. Annoyed, the Spaniards sailed ten miles further upriver to raid the town. The English were caught completely off-guard and only learned of the enemy's arrival by the booming of cannon fire from their ships and the popping of musketry from an advancing expeditionary force that had been put ashore below the town. Brunswick's residents grabbed what few possessions they could carry and fled in terror into the surrounding woods, abandoning the town.

For three days the Spaniards pillaged Brunswick before the English retaliated. Captain William Dry of the Brunswick militia organized a force of about eighty townsmen, sailors, slaves and other armed men from the Lower Cape Fear and counterattacked. Dry's force killed and captured about forty Spaniards onshore and drove the survivors back to their ships. In the ensuing ship-to-shore battle, the *Fortuna* caught fire and blew up, killing her captain, Vincent Lopez, and most of her crew. Stunned by their losses, the Spaniards in the *Loretta* retreated from the Cape Fear, leaving the victorious English again in control of their town. Brunswick's recovery was aided by an auction or sale of goods salvaged from the wreck of the *Fortuna*. Today the only known surviving souvenir taken off the

A 1930s-era watercolor by the late Wilmington artist Henry MacMillan depicting Sloop Point Plantation, built about 1726 on Virginia Creek in the Lower Cape Fear, making it the oldest standing house in North Carolina.

COURTESY OF CHRIS E. FONVIELLE, JR.

Spanish vessel is an oil portrait of Jesus Christ wearing the crown of thorns called *Ecce Homo* (Behold the Man).

The Spaniards wreaked havoc in Brunswick, but natural disasters caused far greater damage. Destructive hurricanes in 1761 and 1769 leveled homes and businesses and disrupted trade and commerce. The 1761 storm was so powerful that it carved a new inlet, appropriately named New Inlet, through a narrow sand spit called the "Haulover" between the ocean and the river about seven miles southeast of Brunswick. Evidence suggests that the 1769 hurricane caused even more destruction at Brunswick and the surrounding area. But neither European enemies nor hurricanes obliterated Brunswick. That feat was unintentionally accomplished by a rival town that soon emerged sixteen miles further up the Cape Fear River.

In 1732, John Watson received from the Crown a warrant for 640 acres of land on the east side of the Cape Fear River, adjacent to its confluence with the Northeast Cape Fear and twenty-eight miles from where the waterway emptied into the Atlantic Ocean at Old Inlet. Soon thereafter, Watson sold three hundred acres of his tract to James Wimble, who planned to build a town called New Carthage. Wimble began selling lots on April 16, 1733, the day historians mark as the beginning of Wilmington. Watson also continued his real estate venture by selling additional lots from his original tract to Michael Higgins and Joshua Grainger.

Late in April 1733, Watson, Wimble, Higgins, and Grainger decided to pool their resources and create a town from their combined holdings. The founders believed that the site at the point where the two rivers met was ideal for a trading center for planters and farmers up and down both waterways. They soon laid out a town called New Liverpool, but from the beginning of settlement residents referred to it as the "New Town" to differentiate it from the old town of Brunswick. The name New Town morphed into Newton by 1734, while Brunswick came to be known as Old Brunswick. Even today Cape Fearians generally refer to Brunswick as Old Brunswick or Brunswick Town.

The site of New Liverpool covered roughly three hundred acres along the riverfront and up a sloping sand ridge to a high plateau, with the town's eastern border being present-day Fifth Avenue but originally called Boundary Street. The town area was divided into square blocks separated by named streets running perpendicular to the river and numbered streets running parallel to the waterway. The

Above: After repulsing a Spanish attack on Brunswick Town in 1748, residents salvaged this portrait of Jesus Christ, called Ecce Homo, *from the captain's cabin of the Spanish sloop* Fortuna *in the Cape Fear River.*

COURTESY OF ST. JAMES CHURCH.

Right: Wilmington was named for Spencer Compton, earl of Wilmington, lord president of His Majesty's Council under King George II of Great Britain, and patron of North Carolina Royal Governor Gabriel Johnston.

COURTESY OF THE NEW HANOVER COUNTY PUBLIC LIBRARY.

main thoroughfare, Market Street, ran eastward and was crossed by Third Street three blocks from the river. Like Brunswick Town, the development of Newton was slow with only a few houses built there within the first couple of years. The village finally began to flourish, however, after Gabriel Johnston became governor of North Carolina in 1734.

Johnston, who would serve as chief executive of the colony for eighteen consecutive years, was sworn in at Brunswick Town and met there with his council for several months. By the spring of 1735, however, Johnston had a falling-out with "the Family" over what he considered their unscrupulous land acquisition deals. From that point on he turned his attention to Newton, using his executive powers to obtain privileges for the town from the Crown and actively promote its development over that of Brunswick Town. The governor set up a land office in Newton, where he personally bought land and encouraged his friends to do the same. He instructed that a courthouse be built in Newton and that the courts convene there. The governor also moved his council meetings from Brunswick Town to Newton and, beginning in 1736, he worked to get official confirmation for the new town. The Brunswick contingent protested but to no avail.

The governor finally got his wish when, on February 25, 1739, the North Carolina General Assembly passed an Act of Incorporation for the town of Wilmington. Johnston had Newton's name changed to commemorate his English patron, Spencer Compton, earl of Wilmington, and lord president of His Majesty's Council under King George II. The Wilmington Act conferred upon the town the right to representation in the colonial assembly and created a board of town commissioners. James Murray, John Porter, and Richard Eagles were among the first board members. Murray was one of the leading merchants in town and the Eagles family owned a large island where they grew rice and which still bears the family name on the west side of the Cape Fear River. Johnston's endeavor to make Wilmington the colony's capital ended in failure when New Bern, centrally located

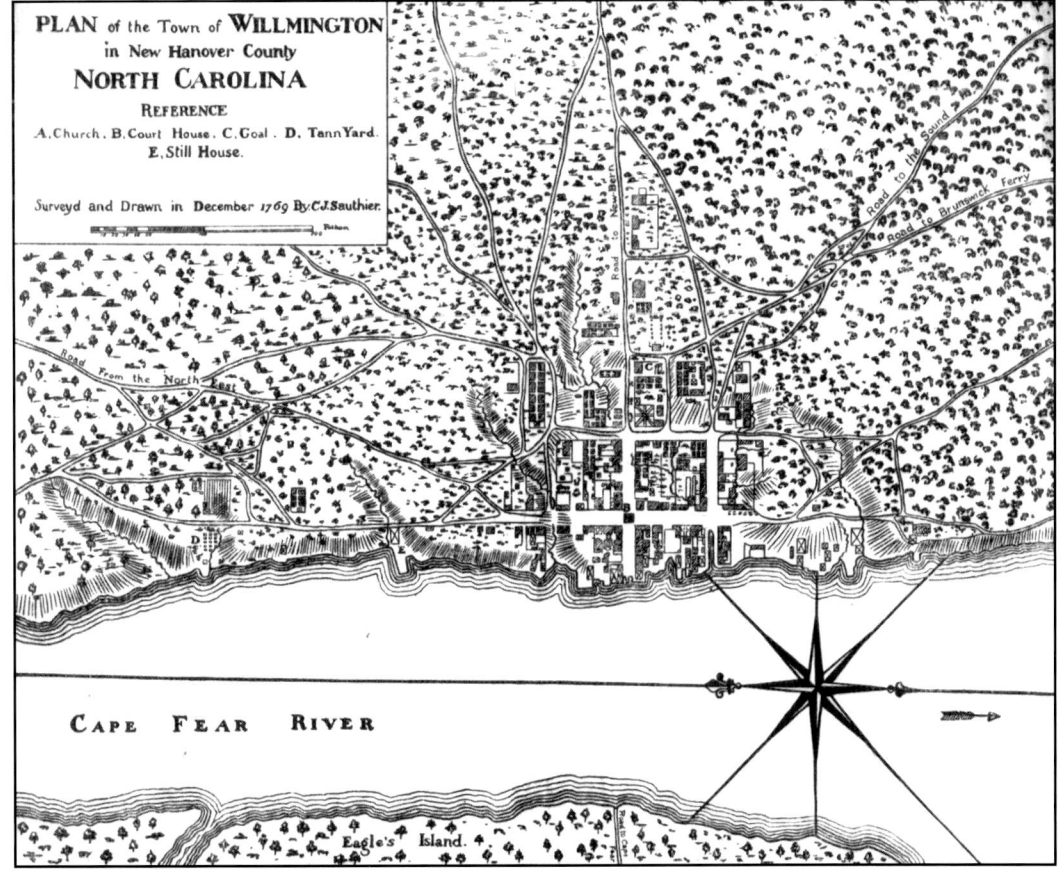

✧

A survey map of the town of Wilmington in 1769 by the British royal cartographer C. J. Sauthier. Note the several streams that cut the landscape from east to west before emptying into the Cape Fear River.
COURTESY OF THE NEW HANOVER COUNTY PUBLIC LIBRARY.

between Wilmington and Edenton, became the official seat of government.

Nevertheless, the Cape Fear quickly became the fastest growing region in North Carolina. The settlers arrived individually and in groups from the Carolinas, Virginia, England, Scotland, Barbados, Pennsylvania, and Massachusetts. Having heard of the opening of the province, they came to take advantage of readily available land and economic opportunities. Benjamin Franklin noted in his *Pennsylvania Gazzette* that "the new settlement going forward at Cape Fear is the subject of much discourse [with] great numbers resorting thither continually from Pennsylvania and other Provinces." The Porters, Lillingtons, Howes, and other prominent families were early arrivals, obtaining land and fanning out along the Cape Fear River and its tributaries.

In September 1739, a large body of Highland Scots arrived in the region and, after remaining in Wilmington for a time, moved up the Cape Fear River to found Cross Creek, Campbellton, Argyle, Manchester and other small communities. More Scots and

✧

Above: According to local tradition, sailors on board vessels coming up the Cape Fear River in olden times hoisted a celebratory dram as they passed this ancient cypress tree. Located on the waterway's east bank a couple of miles below Wilmington, the "Dram Tree" survived until 1941 when it was destroyed to make way for the expansion of the North Carolina Shipbuilding Company.
COURTESY OF THE LOWER CAPE FEAR HISTORICAL SOCIETY.

Right: Built in 1738, the Mitchell-Anderson house on the southeast corner of Front and Orange Streets is the oldest building in Wilmington.
COURTESY OF THE LOWER CAPE FEAR HISTORICAL SOCIETY AND WM. EDMUND BARRETT.

Scots-Irish would immigrate to the sand hills of the upper Cape Fear River valley area until just before the outbreak of the American Revolution. By 1754 some seventy white families lived in Wilmington while only twenty resided in Brunswick Town. The population of New Hanover Precinct in 1742, which would have included what is today Brunswick County, reportedly was three thousand people, two out of every three of whom were black slaves. Indeed, great numbers of Africans also came to the Cape Fear, brought forcibly from Africa by way of colonial islands in the Caribbean Sea and South Carolina.

John Burgwin was typical of Wilmington's early white settlers. The young nineteen-year-old left his hometown of Hereford, England, to seek his fortune in America after his father left his estate to an older brother. Burgwin found employment with Hooper, Alexander & Company, a shipping firm with offices in London, Charleston, and Wilmington. He arrived in Wilmington by 1751, and soon became ensconced as a commission merchant and engaged to Margaret Haynes, the daughter of the Reverend Richard Marsden of St. James Anglican Church.

Burgwin was active in both professional and public life in Wilmington and the colony. He owned a successful mercantile business, importing goods from England and exporting natural resources from Wilmington. After his marriage to Haynes in 1753, Burgwin assumed ownership from his father-in-law of a substantial rice, indigo, and corn plantation called the Hermitage on Prince George's Creek seven miles north of Wilmington. Burgwin's growing fortune enabled him to build an opulent town home on the southwest corner of Third and Market Streets. He was also active in politics, serving as commissioner of Wilmington, clerk of the governor's council, and later member of the General Assembly.

Above: English-born John Burgwin became a successful merchant and property owner after settling in Wilmginton by 1751. Twenty years later he built a magnificent town home, known today as the Burgwin—Wright House, that still stands on the southwest corner of Third and Market Streets.

COURTESY OF THE NORTH CAROLINA MUSEUM OF ART, RALEIGH, GIFT IN MEMORY OF JUDGE W. H. SUMMER BURGWYN AND HIS WIFE, JOSEPHINE GRIFFIN BURGWYN, BY THEIR CHILDREN AND GRANDCHILDREN.

Below: From the beginning of settlement in the Lower Cape Fear, the naval stores industry was a mainstay of the local economy. Pine trees were tapped for crude turpentine which could be distilled into tar and pitch at local facilities. The Lower Cape Fear soon became England's main supplier of naval stores products.

COURTESY OF CHRIS E. FONVIELLE, JR

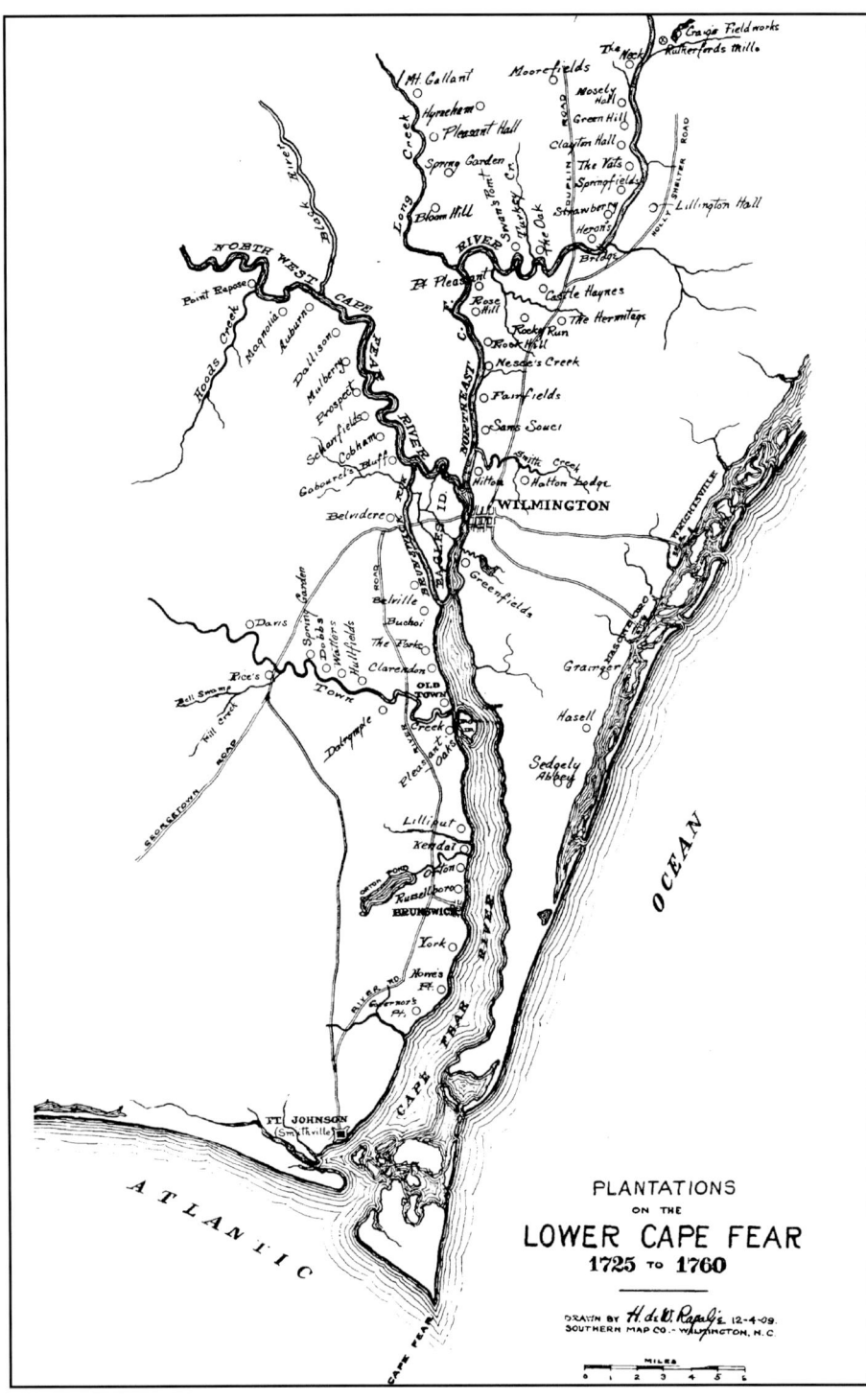

A map of plantations in colonial Cape Fear.
COURTESY OF THE LOWER CAPE FEAR HISTORICAL SOCIETY.

As the revolutionary crisis ensued in the early 1770s, Burgwin found himself torn between loyalty to his homeland and that of his adopted land. Ill treatment for a severely broken leg suffered while playing a game of "blind man's bluff" at the Hermitage in early January 1775, compelled Burgwin to seek treatment in England, just as the Revolutionary War erupted in America. He spent the war years in England and on the continent and consequently lost much of his Cape Fear property to confiscation by the Patriots. Burgwin returned to Wilmington in 1784, successfully reclaimed his holdings, and resumed his mercantile business until his death in 1803.

As Burgwin's story reveals, life along the Cape Fear River in colonial days revolved mostly around planting, shipping, and mercantilism. The region's abundant natural resources—the land, the forests, and the river—dictated economic pursuits. Cape Fearians worked the forests, taking down hardwood trees for ship construction material, barrel staves, and shingles, while pine trees were tapped for resin or crude turpentine. So dense was the Cape Fear's pine forests that the region soon became the British empire's main source of naval stores products—turpentine, tar, and pitch. Area planters grew rice and indigo, much like their cousins in South Carolina. The Cape Fear was as far north as planters could cultivate rice as the region offered plentiful marshes and fresh water for flooding the fields. They also planted corn and beans and raised livestock for export.

Conversely, Cape Fearians imported manufactured products all of kinds that they could not produce themselves. The Cape Fear became an official port of entry in the colony as early as 1731, with all vessels entering and exiting the harbor required to clear at Brunswick Town. The area was officially known as Port Brunswick until 1789 when it was changed to Port Wilmington. Clearly, there was intense rivalry between Brunswick Town and Wilmington over shipping and reflected the great dependence of local trade on the Cape Fear River. Local products and produce were brought to Wilmington on small craft using the Northeast Cape Fear River and upper reaches of the Cape Fear River and their tributaries before being sent downriver to Brunswick Town to be exported to worldwide markets in large ocean-going ships. Imports flowed in the opposite direction.

Despite the emerging competition between Brunswick Town and Wilmington, the two towns depended upon each other for economic survival. The Revolutionary War would change all that, however, with only one town emerging triumphant by war's end.

CHAPTER IV

THE WAR FOR LIBERTY

The grave of Cornelius Harnett and a large monument to him stand only fifty feet apart in historic downtown Wilmington. A beautifully inscribed piece of sandstone marks his final resting place near the northeast corner of St. James Episcopal Church's cemetery while a thirty-foot-tall Connecticut granite obelisk, erected by the North Carolina Society of the Colonial Dames of America in the State of North Carolina in 1906 at the intersection of Fourth and Market Streets, honors Harnett and other colonial heroes of the Lower Cape Fear. People today drive or walk past both markers with perhaps little regard for them or the man they commemorate, but Cornelius Harnett in his day was one of the most influential and respected Patriots in the American cause of independence. Dubbed by Josiah Quincy "the Samuel Adams of North Carolina," Harnett was the foremost defender of liberty in the colony.

Cornelius Harnett was born on April 20, 1723, probably in Chowan County, North Carolina, but moved with his family to the Lower Cape Fear when he was three years old. His father, Cornelius Harnett, Sr., bought the first two lots in Brunswick Town from Maurice Moore, so the young Harnett and the Cape Fear region matured together. His first recorded public service came in 1748 when the Spanish attacked Brunswick Town and he joined the militia force led by William Dry that turned back the invaders. Harnett moved to Wilmington shortly thereafter, as did other residents of Brunswick Town, to take advantage of greater economic opportunities. He soon became a prosperous merchant, his financial success reflected in the purchase of a beautiful piece of property at the confluence of the Northeast Cape Fear River and Smith's Creek one mile north of Wilmington where he built one of the finest plantations in the region that he called Maynard (it was renamed Hilton by its new owner, John Hill, in 1784). Harnett was soon elected commissioner of

✧

This thirty-foot tall Connecticut granite obelisk, erected by the North Carolina Society of the Colonial Dames of America in the State of North Carolina in 1906 at the intersection of Fourth and Market Streets in downtown Wilmington, honors Cornelius Harnett and other colonial heroes of the Lower Cape Fear. The photograph was taken about 1909.

COURTESY OF ALFRED MOORE WADDELL, *HISTORY OF NEW HANOVER COUNTY AND THE LOWER CAPE FEAR REGION, 1723-1800.*

✧

Above: Cornelius Harnett, the most ardent defender of liberty in North Carolina during the American Revolution, lived in this imposing plantation house at the confluence of the Northeast Cape Fear River and Smith's Creek just north of Wilmington. Photographed by Rufus Morgan in 1873, the house survived until 1892, when it was torn down in the name of progress.
COURTESY OF LOWER CAPE FEAR HISTORICAL SOCIETY.

Right: Remains of the ballast stone foundation of Russellborough (also known as Castle Tryon), the home of North Carolina royal governor William Tryon near Brunswick Town, and the site of armed resistance to the Stamp Act by the Cape Fear Sons of Liberty in February 1766.
COURTESY OF CHRIS E. FONVIELLE, JR.

Wilmington, a post he held for twenty-one years, and also served as a justice of the peace and a delegate to the provincial Assembly.

Harnett was best known for his leading role in the revolutionary crisis between the colonies and Great Britain in the 1760s and 1770s. In the aftermath of their victory in the French and Indian War, King George III and Parliament sought to reorganize the vastly expanded American empire. To finance colonial homeland security and pay down its large war debt, the mother country imposed taxes on the colonies, beginning with the Sugar Act in 1764, and the Stamp Act the following year. More than burdensome taxes, the colonials viewed them as egregious violations of their political rights as Englishmen, with their cry being "no taxation without representation." The Lower Cape Fear, a hub of commercial activity in North Carolina and therefore hard hit by the new regulations, soon became the center of opposition to royal authority in the colony, with Cornelius Harnett as the leader.

During the autumn and winter of 1765-1766, residents of the Lower Cape Fear expressed their disapproval of the Stamp Act in several notable public events. On October 19, hundreds of Wilmingtonians gathered to burn in effigy a prominent citizen who favored the new law. Two weeks later, the night before the Stamp Act was to take effect on November 1, a crowd assembled at the St. James Churchyard cemetery to bury an effigy of "Liberty," only to discover that she still "lived." Disgruntled citizens also forced the resignation of the local Stamp Receiver, Dr. William Houston. Governor William Tryon's attempts to quell the civil disorders through mediation and an offer to personally defray some of the stamp tax burden met with derision and refusal.

The Stamp Act crisis in the region came to a head in February 1766, when Captain Jacob Lobb of HMS *Diligence* detained two merchant vessels for failing to carry stamped manifest documents. When the colony's attorney general ruled that the ships should be sent to the vice-admiralty court in Halifax, Nova Scotia, for adjudication, Cape Fear residents responded with anger. Hundreds of men organized as the Sons of Liberty and, on February 19, 1766, marched to confront Governor Tryon at his residence at Castle Tryon (formerly Russellborough) near Brunswick Town. Although the executive refused to be intimidated, the group of armed citizens, including Cornelius Harnett, took possession of the two ships and forced royal customs officials William Pennington and William Dry to renounce their duty to issue stamps. Tryon considered requesting British

military assistance to put down the insurgency, but backed off when Parliament, under considerable political pressure, repealed the Stamp Act in March 1766. The response by the Cape Fear Sons of Liberty to the Stamp Act was the first overt act of opposition to the British government in North Carolina.

War between the colonies and the Crown was barely averted over the Stamp Act crisis and tensions ran high as Parliament continued to pass additional laws in an effort to raise revenue. Residents of the Cape Fear joined with other colonists in boycotting the importation and purchase of English goods. They also displayed their solidarity with Bostonians during the tea conflict of 1773-1774 by sending provisions and supplies to the beleaguered citizens of that port town, while Wilmington ladies reportedly destroyed their own stocks of English tea.

In 1773, Josiah Quincy of Boston toured American towns along the east coast to enlist support for the burgeoning revolutionary cause. He visited Wilmington in late March, meeting with Cornelius Harnett, Robert Howe, a prominent Brunswick County planter, and William Hooper. Quincy encouraged Harnett, with whom he was much impressed, to lead the opposition in North Carolina.

Along with Harnett, William Hooper emerged as a leader of the American cause in North Carolina. Born in Boston and educated at Harvard, Hooper had moved to Wilmington in 1764 to practice law. He soon entered provincial politics, representing New Hanover County in the General Assembly from 1773 until the outbreak of the Revolution. When Massachusetts requested an intercolonial congress to meet in Philadelphia in 1774, Wilmingtonians, headed by Hooper, gathered on July 21 to encourage North Carolinians to meet and select representatives to attend the continental assembly. Heeding the call from Wilmington, the First Provisional Congress of North Carolina met independent of royal authority in New Bern on August 25, 1774. William Hooper, Richard Caswell, and Joseph Hewes were elected as representatives to the First Continental Congress that met in Philadelphia in September 1774. The colonies affirmed their grievances with the Crown and agreed to act together to resolve them, in part by maintaining their policy of economic boycott.

In the autumn of 1774, Cornelius Harnett organized and presided over the Wilmington Committee of Safety to see that the wishes of the Continental Congress were carried out in the Cape Fear. The Committee also supervised preparations for a defensive war, should war come, by training militia forces and stockpiling muskets, gunpowder, and ammunition. Such measures began in earnest after news of the Battles of Lexington and Concord in Massachusetts reached the Wilmington area in early May 1775.

Royal government in North Carolina collapsed soon after the Revolutionary War began. William Tryon, who had become governor of New York in 1771, was succeeded by Josiah Martin, a former British military officer. Martin took a firm stance toward Whigs in North Carolina, dissolving the General Assembly in early April 1775 when it became apparent that he and the Crown had lost the support of most of its members. When a group of Whigs audaciously seized cannon from the grounds of the governor's palace in New Bern, Martin, fearing for his family's

❖

William Hooper of Wilmington represented North Carolina as a delegate to the Continental Congress and was a signer of the Declaration of Independence in Philadelphia. His residence, which survived destruction until 1882, stood on the east side of Second Street about halfway up the block between Market and Princess Streets in Wilmington.

COURTESY OF CHRIS E. FONVIELLE, JR., AND STEVE MCALLISTER.

Hooper's Residence

safety, decided it was time to get out. He sent his wife and children to New York while he sought refuge on board the British sloop-of-war *Cruizer* anchored off Fort Johnston near the mouth of the Cape Fear River.

Martin's appearance in the Cape Fear by early June 1775 was cause for concern among local Patriots, who feared that the region might become a staging area for British military operations and slave revolts. In a show of force, Colonel Robert Howe led five hundred militiamen in an attack on Fort Johnston on July 19, 1775, and burned it to the ground. Ensconced on ships offshore, Governor Martin and the fort's small garrison, commanded by Captain John Collett, were powerless to halt the destruction. Colonel Howe was rewarded for his aggressive action when the Second North Carolina Provisional Congress, which met at Hillsboro in August 1775 to create a provisional government to replace the now defunct royal government, appointed him commander of the Second Regiment North Carolina Continental Troops as of September 1, 1775. James Moore of New Hanover was put in command of the First Regiment. Both men later received commissions as general officers in the Continental Army.

Josiah Martin denounced the revolutionaries and, determined not to relinquish North Carolina to rabble-rousers like Howe, Moore, Harnett, and Hooper, contrived a grand strategy to regain control of his lost colony. Martin believed that Highland Scots, who had sworn allegiance to the King in order to emigrate to America and acquire land in the upper Cape Fear River valley, would rally to the royal standard if called upon. With these Scots and other Loyalists assisting regular British troops, the governor would invade North Carolina by way of the Cape Fear River. Indeed, Martin asked the imperial government to send ten thousand well-armed soldiers and artillery as the nucleus of his mighty army. The Colonial

✧

Above: Colonel Robert Howe of Brunswick County commanded the Second Regiment North Carolina Continental Troops after September 1, 1775, and was later commissioned a major general in the Continental Army.
COURTESY OF THE LOWER CAPE FEAR HISTORICAL SOCIETY.

Below: The first military engagement of the American Revolution in North Carolina took place at Moore's Creek Bridge near Wilmington on February 27, 1776, pitting American Patriots against American Loyalists. Colonel Richard Caswell commanded eight hundred Patriot militiamen in the battle.
COURTESY OF CHRIS E. FONVIELLE, JR.

Secretary Lord Dartmouth believed that Martin's plan was overly-optimistic, but he ultimately agreed to it and made arrangements for troops to be dispatched from Ireland and New England.

The stage was now set for Martin's invasion and he soon put his plan into motion. On January 10, 1776, he issued a proclamation calling on Loyalists to "put down the unnatural and horrid rebellion" and restore North Carolina to the Crown. He promised two hundred acres of land and tax exemption for twenty years in return for their services if the campaign proved successful. He requested that they mobilize and rendezvous with British forces at Brunswick Town by February 15. Martin commissioned Donald MacDonald as a brigadier general to command the Loyalist forces and Donald McLeod as a lieutenant colonel and second in command. MacDonald and McLeod recruited sixteen hundred Loyalists mostly from Cross Creek and Campbelltown in Cumberland County, and began to march down the Cape Fear River—three days after Martin had planned for them to arrive at Brunswick Town.

American Patriots learned of Martin's ploy and moved to intercept MacDonald and McLeod's slow moving army. They discovered an ideal spot at which to block the Loyalists' line of march about twenty miles northwest of Wilmington at widow Elizabeth Moore's bridge on Moore's Creek, a tributary of the Black River that flows into the Cape Fear. Colonel Alexander Lillington occupied the position with 150 militiamen on February 25 and constructed breastworks on a knoll along the east bank of the narrow stream. Colonel Richard Caswell soon arrived with eight hundred militia reinforcements, while Colonel James Moore and the First Regiment North Carolina Continentals deployed on the Cape Fear River.

Having failed to elude the Patriots, MacDonald and McLeod believed they had little choice but to attempt to overrun Lillington and Caswell's position at Moore's Creek Bridge if they hoped to advance to Brunswick Town. They attacked before sunrise on February 27, 1776. McLeod personally led the assault as the elderly MacDonald was too ill to leave his encampment in the rear. With bagpipes playing in the background, cheering Highland warriors advanced through the pre-dawn darkness with their broadswords drawn and muskets primed. The bridge impeded their advance, however, as it had been sabotaged by the Patriots who had removed most of its planking and greased the stringers with animal tallow and soft soap. A vanguard of Scottish broadswordsmen, commanded by Captain John Campbell, was gingerly making its way across the girders when the Patriots opened fire with muskets and two cannon named "Mother Covington and her daughter." Heavy volleys of lead musket balls and artillery canister killed both McLeod and Campbell and about forty of their men and routed the survivors. The Highlanders offered only a feeble response that cut down two Patriots, one of whom, John Grady of Duplin County, received a mortal wound. Colonel Moore and his Continental troops arrived a few hours after the battle and organized a pursuit of the Loyalists, capturing

✧

Above: Colonel Alexander Lillington's Patriot troops constructed these earthworks, now eroded by time and the elements, to defend Moore's Creek Bridge in 1776. The serenity of Moore's Creek National Battlefield in a lowland swamp and pine barren belies the fighting that took place there 231 years ago.
COURTESY OF LARRY USILTON.

Below: A diorama in the visitor center at Moore's Creek National Battlefield depicts Highland-Scot Loyalist troops led by Lieutenant Colonel Donald McLeod and Captain John Campbell coming under fire by Patriots defending Moore's Creek Bridge.
COURTESY OF MOORE'S CREEK NATIONAL BATTLEFIELD.

General MacDonald and most of his men as well as valuable arms and ammunition.

The Battle of Moore's Creek Bridge, one of the first military engagements of the American Revolution in the South, lasted only about fifteen minutes, but it proved to be of great importance. It allowed the Patriots to consolidate control of the Cape Fear, diminished Loyalist sentiment in southeastern North Carolina, and stifled British military operations in the South for almost three years. More importantly, it emboldened North Carolinians to support the growing independence movement that had been so eloquently articulated in Thomas Paine's *Common Sense*, published only one month before Moore's Creek. Five weeks after the battle, the Fourth North Carolina Provincial Congress met in Halifax to consider actions against King George III. On April 12, 1776, delegates unanimously passed the Halifax Resolves which emphasized North Carolinians commitment to independence. The Resolves dictated that "the Delegates for this Colony in the Continental Congress be empowered to Concur with the Delegates of the other Colonies in declaring Independence…." Cornelius Harnett, representing Wilmington, chaired the committee that wrote the Halifax Resolves, the first official statement on independence by a colony. When the Continental Congress adopted a national Declaration of Independence in Philadelphia the following July, William Hooper of Wilmington signed it.

As North Carolina moved toward independence in the aftermath of the Battle of Moore's Creek Bridge, the long awaited British soldiers sent to lead Josiah Martin's grand invasion of the colony finally reached the Cape Fear. A small force commanded by Major General Henry Clinton arrived at the end of March 1776, followed in early May by forty-five hundred redcoats under Major General Charles Cornwallis. With no force of Loyalists to assist them, however, they busied themselves by marauding up and down the Cape Fear River. Although they never seriously threatened Wilmington, the British burned Orton mill and plundered Kendal, one of Robert Howe's plantations near Brunswick Town. Clinton and Cornwallis finally resolved to abandon the Cape Fear to go after Charleston, South Carolina, and so, accompanied by a frustrated Josiah Martin, sailed away in late May 1776. They left behind several warships to blockade Wilmington and at least one regiment of soldiers to occupy the Cape Fear estuary.

The enemy's continued presence and activities were a source of apprehension and irritation to residents of the Lower Cape Fear. The British persisted in their raids of farms and plantations along the river, terrorizing residents, seizing livestock and provisions, and freeing slaves. They also pillaged and allegedly burned Brunswick Town. Provoked, the Americans soon retaliated.

In early September 1776, a Patriot expeditionary force mobilized at Snow's Point below Brunswick Town for an assault on Bald Head Island. Its target was Fort George, a palisade work built by British occupation troops on the west end of Bald Head. Ferried across the river on transports, 150 Americans commanded by a "Colonel Poke," made landfall at Buzzard's Bay, marched down present day East Beach, and then turned westward to attack Fort George. The fort's garrison managed to repulse the assault with the assistance of British warships *Cruizer*, *Falcon*, and *Scorpion* that bombarded the Americans from their anchorage near the mouth of the river. As the Patriots attempted to retreat back across the river, British naval forces came upstream to intercept them. After a heavy exchange of cannon fire, however, the British withdrew. Occurring only

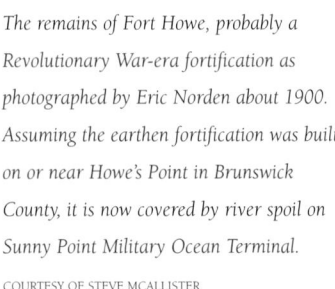

The remains of Fort Howe, probably a Revolutionary War-era fortification as photographed by Eric Norden about 1900. Assuming the earthen fortification was built on or near Howe's Point in Brunswick County, it is now covered by river spoil on Sunny Point Military Ocean Terminal.
COURTESY OF STEVE MCALLISTER.

two months after the signing of the Declaration of Independence, the Battle of Bald Head Island may have been the first amphibious operation in United States military history.

The Cape Fear largely escaped the horrors of war after British forces finally departed the area by early November 1776, although British privateers preyed on American vessels offshore, occasionally shutting down trade and shipping. The destruction of Fort Johnston had left the region largely defenseless, and Cape Fearians were fortunate the British army did not return for more than four years. Residents evacuated Brunswick Town for havens upriver and in the countryside. In fact, the town was not even represented in the new state's General Assembly, and in 1779 the seat of Brunswick County's government was moved to a safer location at Lockwood's Folly, further weakening the once thriving port.

With the war going badly for the British in the northern part of the country by 1778, they shifted military operations back to the South. In late December of that year, they captured Savannah, Georgia, which had been defended by Major General Robert Howe, commander of the Department of the South. In mid-May 1780, Lieutenant General Henry Clinton and Lieutenant General Charles Earl Cornwallis were victorious after a long siege of Charleston, South Carolina, which they had failed to take four years earlier. In 1781, Cornwallis led his crimson-uniformed army into North Carolina hoping to encourage Loyalists and slaves to support his invasion and help him defeat a Patriot army under Major General Nathanael Greene. The two armies clashed at Guilford Couthouse on March 15, 1781, in what turned out to be the largest Revolutionary War battle in North Carolina. The British carried the day on the battlefield but were so badly bloodied and short on supplies that Cornwallis determined to retreat to Wilmington on the coast.

Key to Cornwallis's campaign in North Carolina was the capture of Wilmington, which would give him a base to refit, recover, and rest his army under the protection of the navy. When Cornwallis advanced into the interior of the state, Major James H. Craig sailed up the coast from Charleston with about four hundred British troops, most of them musket-bearers of the Eighty-second Regiment of Foot, to attack Wilmington. On January 28, 1781, Craig's unit and a contingent of Royal Marines landed at Ellis Plantation nine miles south of Wilmington and marched upstream, with warships providing covering fire from the river. The British captured the town without opposition as many Patriots fled, Cornelius Harnett and William Hooper among them. While soldiers set about fortifying the sand hills below the town, Major Craig coerced citizens who remained behind to sign an oath of allegiance to the king. He also impounded the property of dissidents and exiled their families including Ann Clark Hooper, wife of William Hooper, and her children.

One of Craig's main objectives was to round up prominent rebel leaders. The major personally led a party to search for the most wanted man—Cornelius Harnett. After fleeing Wilmington, Harnett had taken refuge at the house of James Spicer in Onslow County. Too ill to continue his flight, however, Harnett was discovered and

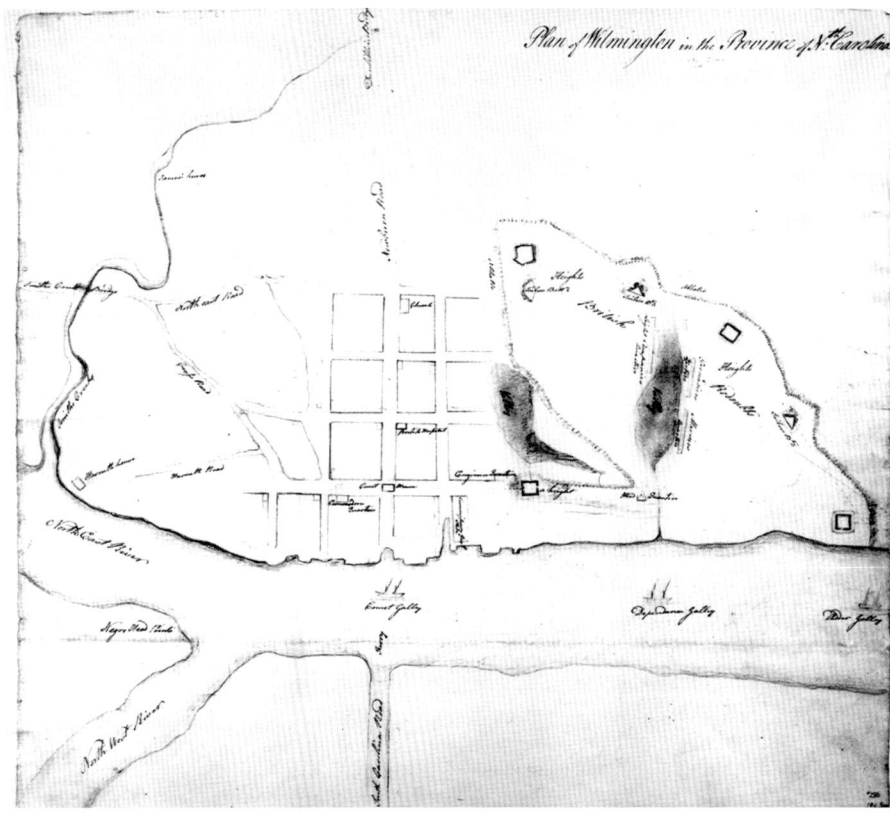

❖

Above: A sketch map of British defenses and ships at Wilmington during Major James H. Craig's occupation of the town in 1781.
COURTESY OF THE LOWER CAPE FEAR HISTORICAL SOCIETY.

Below: An iron cannonball, lead musket and pistol balls, silver knee buckles, a pewter British military uniform button of the Eighty-second Regiment of Foot, and a silver piece of eight Spanish real found in a Revolutionary War encampment on the Northeast Cape Fear River.
COURTESY OF CHRIS E. FONVIELLE, JR.

Above: For eighteen days in April 1781, British Lieutenant General Charles Earl Cornwallis reportedly made his headquarters in the home of John Burgwin at Third and Market Streets in Wilmington. The structure, now known as the Burgwin-Wright House, has been owned since 1937 by the National Society of the Colonial Dames of America in the State of North Carolina.
COURTESY OF THE NEW HANOVER COUNTY PUBLIC LIBRARY.

Below: The Burgwin-Wright House recently acquired a document authorizing payments to British soldiers that was signed by General Cornwallis and postdated Wilmington, April 15, 1781.
COURTESY OF THE NATIONAL SOCIETY OF THE COLONIAL DAMES OF AMERICA IN THE STATE OF NORTH CAROLINA.

arrested. Craig allegedly had Harnett tied up and thrown over the back of a horse "like a sack of meal" for the forty-mile-long trek back to Wilmington. After reaching the town, Harnett was imprisoned in a roofless blockhouse where poor health and exposure to the elements doomed him. Upon Harnett's death in April 1781, his body was buried in the cemetery behind St. James Church. John Ashe, a general of local militia, was also apprehended and died in captivity.

The arrest of Harnett initiated what local tradition claims was a reign of terror by Major Craig. Cruel though it may have been, it was also effective, enabling the British to largely subdue the region by the time Cornwallis arrived in Wilmington on or about April 7, 1781. Strong circumstantial evidence suggests that the commanding general established his headquarters in the home of John Burgwin at Third and Market Streets, which locals still often refer to as the "Cornwallis House." As his army refitted and recuperated, the British commander plotted his next move. Cornwallis's intelligence sources advised him that the Carolinas could not be conquered so long as arms and equipment for General Greene's army were coming out of Virginia. By concentrating his army at the mouth of the Chesapeake Bay, he might well cut off American trade with France and bring the war to a close.

On April 25, 1781, eighteen days after arriving in the Cape Fear, Cornwallis marched his army northward up the coastal plain of North Carolina to his rendezvous with destiny at Yorktown the following October. The general's plans for the ill-fated invasion that led to his ultimate defeat in the American Revolution had been made in Wilmington. There was little reason for Major Craig to remain in Wilmington after news of Cornwallis's surrender to General Washington at Yorktown reached him. The British sailed from the Cape Fear on November 18, 1781.

With the war now over, Wilmingtonians looked to the future. For Brunswick Town, however, there was little future. At war's end the seaport was reportedly "almost wholly demolished and deserted." Archaeological digs in the late 1950s and 1960s suggest that former residents or squatters may have lived at Brunswick Town until about 1840, but the port never recovered from the Revolutionary War and competition from Wilmington.

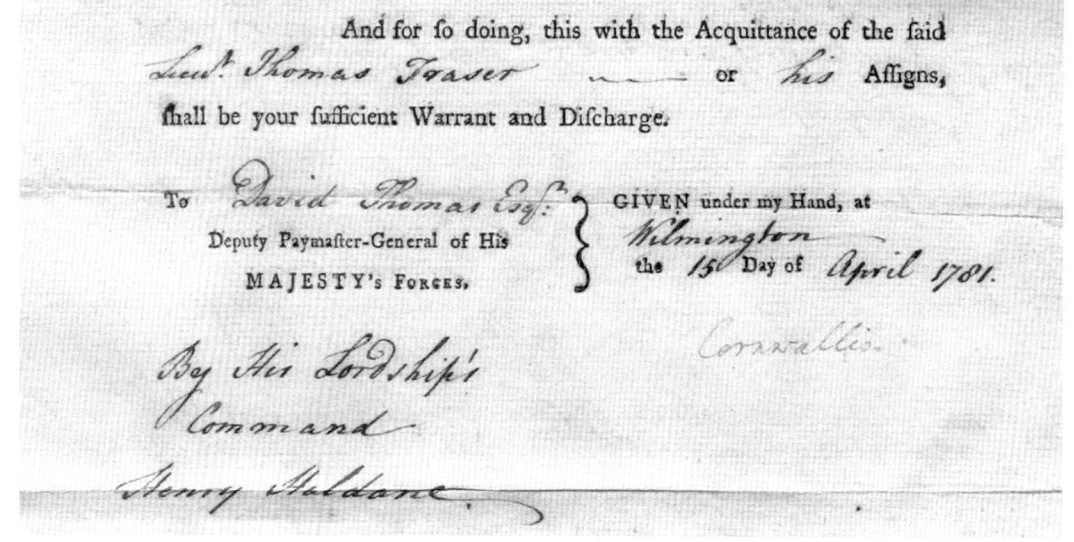

Chapter V

Antebellum Wilmington

Zebulon and William Latimer, natives of Glastonbury, Connecticut, moved to North Carolina in the 1830s, eventually settling in Wilmington by 1839 or 1840. The Latimers typified the many immigrants, especially Northerners and Europeans, who flocked to Wilmington to take advantage of economic opportunities in the rapidly growing port town in the decades before the Civil War. The brothers became partners in a dry goods business called W. & Z. Latimer. Zebulon married Elizabeth Savage of Wilmington in 1843, and soon acquired enough wealth as a merchant to build a palatial residence for his growing family on the northwest corner of Third and Orange Streets. Zebulon Latimer's economic success was shared by many other Wilmingtonians during the antebellum period.

Wilmington emerged as North Carolina's largest town and leading seaport by 1840. Growth and development was uneven until the late 1830s when internal improvements enhanced the port's status and economic opportunities for residents and immigrants alike. Wilmington had never experienced such rampant expansion.

Brunswick Town's demise after the American Revolution left Wilmington as the only urban place in the Lower Cape Fear for a time. As one reporter for *Gleason's Pictorial Drawing Room Companion* observed, "Wilmington, more eligibly situated, first became [Brunswick's] rival and then its gravedigger." As Brunswick Town faded into oblivion, a new town—Smithville—was established near the mouth of the river. Founded and promoted by Joshua Potts of Wilmington, Smithville was named for wealthy Cape Fear landowner and politician Benjamin Smith, the great-grandson of Landgrave Thomas Smith who had received the first land grant in the Cape Fear in 1713. Benjamin Smith married Sarah Dry, daughter of William Dry, the colonial customs officer at Brunswick Town. Smith also served as an aide-de-camp on General George Washington's staff during the Revolutionary War. In the mid-1780s, he embarked on an illustrious political career, representing Brunswick County in the state house for many years before being elected governor in 1810.

Sailing ships approach Wilmington's docks on a placid Cape Fear River.
COURTESY OF THE LOWER CAPE FEAR HISTORICAL SOCIETY.

✧

Above: Zebulon Latimer moved from Connecticut to Wilmington by 1839 or 1840 to take advantage of the town's booming economy. His successful dry goods business in Wilmington enabled him to build this opulent home for his family at Third and Orange Streets in 1852. Today the Latimer House is used as the headquarters for the Lower Cape Fear Historical Society.
COURTESY OF THE LOWER CAPE FEAR HISTORICAL SOCIETY.

Top, right: Many Europeans immigrated to Wilmington in the 1830s-1850s, giving the town a cosmopolitan flavor. Hanke Vollers arrived from Hanover, Germany, and became a Wilmington merchant and member of the German Volunteers, a pre-Civil War militia unit.
COURTESY OF R. VOLLERS HANSON

Below: Benjamin Smith, a wealthy Cape Fear land owner and member of North Carolina's General Assembly, introduced a bill in 1792 for incorporation of a new town near the mouth of the Cape Fear River called Smithville (later renamed Southport), seen here about 1900.
COURTESY OF THE LOWER CAPE FEAR HISTORICAL SOCIETY.

Smith introduced a bill in North Carolina's General Assembly for incorporation of a town adjacent to Fort Johnston, two miles from the mouth of the Cape Fear River. Incorporated in 1792, Smithville emerged as a quaint village whose population of several hundred people comprised mostly soldiers' families, riverboat pilots, and watermen. It also soon became a popular summertime resort and getaway for Wilmingtonians and vacationers who enjoyed the salubrious ocean breezes that blew across the exposed site. In 1889 Smithville was renamed Southport by promoters who hoped to make it the state's southern-most major seaport.

Unlike Brunswick Town, Smithville never rivaled Wilmington for supremacy as the region's leading seaport. For most of its history Smithville remained a small riverside village, largely because it lacked the infrastructure to become a principal port. At the same time, Wilmington power-brokers lobbied federal and state authorities and private donors for funds for much-needed improvements in transportation and communication to enhance their port over Smithville.

Wilmington may have been ideally located for local trade up and down the Cape Fear and Northeast Cape Fear Rivers, but the town's connection to the outside world had depended in large part on Brunswick Town, whose deep anchorage accommodated ocean-going commerce vessels. The river channel north of Brunswick Town was intricate and shallow in places, particularly at the mouth of Town Creek.

Silt flowing down the creek for thousands of years had created a shoal called "the Flats," which only vessels of light draft could cross. Local business suffered as farmers and shippers found it difficult to get their produce and products to markets outside the region. Navigational problems and the absence of good roads posed serious obstacles to progress. The loss of Brunswick Town as the area's international port threatened Wilmington's economic vitality.

As a result, Wilmington's growth was hindered early on. The town grew, but not at a fast pace. Only about twelve hundred residents lived in Wilmington in 1790. The town boasted a population of 2,633 by 1820, but that made it only the fourth largest community in the state behind New Bern (90 miles up the coast), Fayetteville (90 miles up the Cape Fear River), and Raleigh, the state capital. Navigational problems were not the only reason for Wilmington's comparatively slow growth in the early 1800s. Inadequate banking facilities and hotels and destructive fires also stifled Wilmington's expansion. The town also suffered from a reputation as an unhealthy place, as serious yellow fever epidemics wracked the town in 1819 and again in 1821. Even so, poor transportation and communication remained the chief obstacles to development.

The federal government alleviated part of the problem by funding the construction of lighthouses and range lights at the Cape Fear. A lighthouse was built by 1795 on riverfront property on Bald Head Island donated by Benjamin Smith, but erosion forced a replacement beacon to be built. A 110-foot-tall structure dubbed "Old Baldy" was erected on the north end of the island by 1817. Old Baldy guided mariners safely into the harbor by way of Old Inlet, and although no longer used for navigational purposes today, it is the oldest standing lighthouse in North Carolina. Beginning in 1851, a lightship stationed on Frying Pan Shoals, a dangerous reef that stretches eighteen miles into the Atlantic Ocean from Bald Head Island's southeastern-most point, helped seamen avoid wrecking their vessels along the Cape of Fear.

A lighthouse on Federal Point near the tip of New Hanover County helped ships enter the river through New Inlet. A federally-subsidized beacon was operational there as early as 1816, but was replaced by a taller brick tower in 1837. The second lighthouse remained intact until early 1863 when Confederate soldiers dismantled it. Federal funding also led to the placement of a series of buoys and beacons from the mouth of the river all the way to Wilmington. Range lights at Price's Creek and Orton Point on the Brunswick County side of the river, on Campbell Island at the mouth of Town Creek, and at Mt. Tirza three miles south of Wilmington, helped guide ships upstream like a well-lit runway.

The chief concern for improving transportation, however, remained the Cape Fear River itself. As early as 1788 Amaziah Jocelin of Wilmington spearheaded an effort to deepen the channel at the Flats at the mouth of Town Creek. Jocelin's project foundered for lack of funds, but the state government promoted trade in the early 1800s by contracting with companies such as the Cape Fear Navigation Company, chartered in 1811, to improve navigation by removing tree stumps and debris in the river. By the 1830s steam dredges were being used to scoop out

✧

Top, left: Pioneer photographer John Plumbe, Jr. may have taken the earliest known image of Wilmington, showing the Burgwin-Wright House and St. James Episcopal Church at Third and Market Streets, circa 1848.
COURTESY OF THE AMON CARTER MUSEUM FORT WORTH, TEXAS.

Above: Wilmington was ideally situated for local commerce along both the Cape Fear and Northeast Cape Fear Rivers, but internal improvements during antebellum days enhanced its viability as a national seaport.
COURTESY OF THE NEW HANOVER COUNTY PUBLIC LIBRARY.

Below: Old Baldy, North Carolina's oldest standing lighthouse, was built on Bald Head Island at the mouth of the Cape Fear River in 1816-1817.
COURTESY OF CHRIS E. FONVIELLE, JR.

CHAPTER V

❖

Above: The *Prometheus* was one of the first steamboats to ply the Cape Fear River, arriving in 1818 from Swansboro, North Carolina, where she had been built by Otway Burns.
COURTESY OF THE NEW HANOVER COUNTY PUBLIC LIBRARY.

Right: Captain Benjamin W. Beery, along with his brother William, owned and operated a large-scale commercial shipbuilding business on Eagles Island before and during the Civil War.
COURTESY OF THE NEW HANOVER COUNTY PUBLIC LIBRARY.

Below: The steamboat *A. P. Hurt* was built in Wilmington, Delaware, in 1859-1860, as a transport vessel for B. G. and T. C. Worth in Wilmington, North Carolina. Reportedly one of the first steel-hulled steamboats to be constructed in the United States, the *A. P. Hurt* saw service on the Cape Fear River until 1923, when she sank at her moorings at the foot of Dock Street.
COURTESY OF RICHARD LAWRENCE.

sediment silting the channel. New Inlet presented a challenge as sand constantly being pushed by the ocean through the inlet was clogging the channel behind Federal Point. In 1853, the U.S. Corps of Engineers recommended closing New Inlet to traffic, but opponents prevented that from occurring until after the Civil War. Ironically, the government's failure to undertake the proposed project proved to be advantageous to the South during the Civil War, as it provided two passageways into the harbor for Confederate ships.

The arrival of steam transports also aided Wilmington's development as the state's principal seaport and one of the leading ports along the Atlantic seaboard. In 1813, only six years after Robert Fulton took the *Clermont* up the Hudson River in New York, John Stevens of New Jersey received a charter from the North Carolina legislature to operate steamboats on the Cape Fear River. When Stevens failed to take advantage of his five year monopoly, a new contract was awarded to James Seawell, who quickly put two steamboats into operation on the Cape Fear. The *Henrietta*, built in Fayetteville, was the first steamboat to appear on

the waterway at the end of April 1818, followed in mid-October of that year by the *Prometheus*. The *Prometheus* had been constructed in Swansboro, North Carolina by Otway Burns, a successful commerce raider during the War of 1812. Both steamboats made regular runs on the Cape Fear between Wilmington and Fayetteville, but the *Prometheus* also traveled downriver. Her most famous passenger was probably President James Monroe, who rode from Wilmington to Smithville on April 17, 1819.

When Seawell's monopoly expired in 1826, other steamboat companies began shipping in the area. The *Spray*, *A. P. Hurt*, *North Carolina*, and other vessels operating on the river in antebellum days stimulated the growth of Wilmington and its economy as well as that of towns upriver, including Elizabethtown and Fayetteville.

Just as important to Wilmington's explosive growth in the antebellum period was the coming of the railroad. As early as 1833, Wilmingtonians Edward B. Dudley, Alexander MacRae, and William B. Meares attempted to gain state support for a rail line between the seaport and the capital. The following year the legislature chartered the Wilmington & Raleigh

Railroad. Construction began as soon as sufficient funding had been raised through stock sales by October 1836, and intensified after Edward B. Dudley became governor. Dudley, the first governor elected by popular vote in North Carolina and the only Wilmingtonian to ascend to the state's highest office, also happened to be the railroad's first president and largest stock holder.

The corporation's intention to link Wilmington with Raleigh soon changed, however, to a line connecting Wilmington with Virginia as part of a larger plan to build an intra-coastal railroad from New England to Florida. Ultimately, the Wilmington line ran up the coastal plain to Weldon, North Carolina, where it connected to the Petersburg & Weldon Railroad into southeastern Virginia. At 161 1/2 miles long, the Wilmington & Weldon Railroad reportedly was the longest iron road in the world at the time of its completion on March 7, 1840. The line boosted business in Wilmington and enhanced its status as a regional market, with shipments of cotton, flour, bacon, and naval stores increasing as each section of rail was completed. The Wilmington & Weldon Railroad would take on even greater importance during the Civil War.

The success of the Wilmington & Weldon Railroad led to the construction of two additional lines. The Wilmington & Manchester Railroad was incorporated in 1847, with construction beginning two years later. Completed in 1854, the railroad ran southwesterly into South Carolina, indirectly connecting Wilmington to Charleston by way of Fair Bluff, Manchester, and Florence. In 1855, thanks to the efforts of Wilmingtonians Dr. Armand John DeRosset, Henry Nutt, and Robert H. Cowan, the North Carolina legislature chartered the Wilmington, Charlotte & Rutherfordton Railroad. The line traversed the western piedmont counties for trade. By the time the Civil War broke out in 1861, Wilmington was tapped by three railroads and would remain a major railroad depot for both commercial and passenger service for the next century.

Further enhancing the Tar Heel port's development were vast improvements to local roads. In colonial days Wilmington was linked to Georgetown and Charleston, South Carolina by the King's Highway. As early as 1727, Cornelius Harnett, Sr., operated a ferry from Brunswick Town to Sugar Loaf where passengers picked up a road that ran up the sandy east bank of the Cape Fear River to Wilmington. By the 1730s a thoroughfare known as the New Bern Road was laid between Wilmington and the Neuse River. The old New Bern Road was later incorporated into present-day Princess Place Drive. In 1764 town commissioners approved Richard Eagles's request to build a causeway across Eagles Island just opposite Market Street in Wilmington. Two years later Benjamin Heron received permission to construct a drawbridge over the Northeast Cape Fear River, improving the Duplin Road that ran into interior counties of the state. Located at the end of what is today Blossom Ferry Road in Castle Hayne, Heron's Bridge was one of the earliest drawbridges in colonial America. Unless the roads were corduroyed—ribbed with logs laid crosswise and covered with dirt to build up a sufficient road bed—

✧

Above: Wilmingtonian Edward B. Dudley, president and largest stock holder in the Wilmington & Raleigh Railroad, used his power and influence to push construction of the railroad after he was elected governor of North Carolina in 1836. Later renamed the Wilmington & Weldon Railroad, it helped Wilmington become the state's busiest seaport and largest town. The railroad became the main supply route of General Robert E. Lee's Army of Northern Virginia during the Civil War.

COURTESY OF BILL ROBERTS AND THE LOWER CAPE FEAR HISTORICAL SOCIETY.

Below: The construction of better roads in the Lower Cape Fear, including the Federal Point Road between Wilmington and Federal Point at the tip of New Hanover County, brought more people and more trade to Wilmington in the antebellum period.

COURTESY OF THE NEW HANOVER COUNTY PUBLIC LIBRARY.

✧

Above: On any given day in the nineteenth century, Wilmington's docks on both sides of the Cape Fear River, including this wharf on Eagles Island, were lined with hundreds of barrels of naval stores—tar, pitch, and turpentine—awaiting export.
COURTESY OF THE LOWER CAPE FEAR HISTORICAL SOCIETY.

Below: Wilmington's prosperity in the antebellum era was perhaps best symbolized by its imposing private residences and public buildings such as City Hall, built 1855-1858, and which is still used today as both the city's administration offices and public theater.
COURTESY OF THE NEW HANOVER COUNTY PUBLIC LIBRARY.

which was both time consuming and expensive, they rarely traversed swamps and pocosins (known as Carolina bays).

In the late 1840s, Fayetteville and Wilmington initiated the plank road system in North Carolina. Roads paved with planks allowed traffic to pass more easily through low and sandy ground. Chartered in 1849, the Wilmington and Masonboro Plank Road Company improved the road between town and Masonboro Sound. Two years later the Topsail Plank Road Company was established to plank the route between Wilmington and Topsail Sound. Market Street was extended eastward from Thirteenth Street, reconnecting with the old New Bern Road near what is today North 17 Shopping Center. From there the road, generally referred to as the Topsail Sound Plank Road, ran toward Scott's Hill, Topsail Sound, and New Bern.

Internal improvements catapulted Wilmington into the most thriving economic center in North Carolina. By 1840, Wilmington had surpassed New Bern as the most populated town in the state with 4,744 residents. The town's population had doubled since 1820 and would double again by 1860. People rushed to the area from all over to take advantage of the booming economy. John Dawson immigrated from Ireland by 1830, to become owner of a successful dry goods business and mayor of Wilmington. He was soon followed by his brother James who became a prominent banker in town. Brothers John C. and Robert B. Wood arrived from Nantucket, Massachusetts, about 1839, and became the most sought after "master builders" in Wilmington. The Woods constructed many private residences, such as the Zebulon Latimer House, as well as public buildings, including City Hall-Thalian Hall and St. James Church. James Cassidey, a native of Salisbury, Massachusetts, became one of Wilmington's principal shipbuilders before and during the Civil War.

While Cassidey's Shipyard operated in Wilmington, Benjamin and William Beery ran a commercial shipbuilding business on Eagles Island across the river from the downtown district. Beery's Shipyard, known as the Confederate Navy Yard during the Civil War, built and repaired both wooden and iron-hulled steam vessels. Two iron and copper works also thrived in Wilmington—Hart & Polley (later Hart & Bailey) and Clarendon Iron Works (also known as the Thomas E. Roberts Factory). Before the Civil War, however, the Lower Cape Fear's main industry remained in naval stores—tar, pitch, and turpentine from pine resin—for the construction and maintenance of wooden-hulled vessels. During the war cotton eclipsed naval stores and lumber products as the region's main export.

By the end of the antebellum era Wilmington had grown from a modest-size port into North Carolina's largest and busiest seaport, with an active mercantile trade and an impressive array of industry. That would bode well for both the state and the South in the difficult days just ahead.

The Mound Battery at Confederate Fort Fisher under heavy Union naval bombardment in January 1865.
LITHOGRAPHY BY JAMES MADISON ALDEN.

Chapter VI

Wilmington Turned "Topsy-Turvy" by Civil War

The blockade runner *Condor* steamed swiftly toward the entrance of the Cape Fear River at New Inlet in the early morning hours of October 1, 1864. Making her maiden voyage, the *Condor* carried a valuable cargo of military supplies destined for the Confederacy. Her captain, William N. W. Hewett, hoped to get his ship under the guns of Fort Fisher guarding New Inlet before Union blockading ships detected her and gave chase. Suddenly the silhouette of another ship loomed in the darkness straight ahead, forcing the *Condor's* pilot to cut hard to starboard to avoid a collision. It was a fatal mistake as the *Condor* ran hard aground near the beach.

The misfortune did not sway Captain Hewett's confidence that he could free the ship on a rising tide, but some of his passengers did not share his optimism. The *Condor's* most famous rider, the celebrated spy Rose O'Neale Greenhow, feared for her life as she was carrying important dispatches for the Confederate government from diplomats in England. She also had hundreds of gold sovereigns, royalties from the sale of her memoirs penned in England, tucked away in a pouch draped around her neck. Having already spent time in prison for espionage, Greenhow dreaded being captured by Union sailors and returned to jail. She insisted that Captain Hewett get her to shore. Against his better judgment he relented, putting her and two other prominent passengers into a lifeboat to be rowed to the beach by several crewmen. Rough seas capsized the small craft, however, and though the sailors and other travelers made it to safety, Mrs. Greenhow was dragged below the waves and drowned.

A soldier from Fort Fisher, Private J. J. Doc Conner, walking his beat along the shoreline about sunrise found Mrs. Greenhow's bag of gold, which he eventually turned in to his commanding officer, Colonel William Lamb. Thomas Taylor, whose blockade running company owned the stranded vessel, *Night Hawk*, that the Condor had swerved to miss, found Mrs. Greenhow's body washed up on the beach later that morning. Her body was recovered and taken to Wilmington and buried with full military honors in Oakdale Cemetery. Also lost to the sea was the *Condor*, which Captain Hewett was never able to wrest from the sandbar. She remains buried in the ocean off Fort Fisher to this day.

Mrs. Greenhow's tragic death was more than just a story of the loss of one of the most alluring and successful female spies in American history. It also reflected the nature of Confederate blockade running which James Sprunt, a former purser's clerk on board blockade runners and an early chronicler of Cape Fear history, described as both "life preserving and death dealing." The clandestine maritime trade helped the Confederacy sustain its war effort for four years but often at great peril to the people engaged in it and the places exposed to it. It cost Rose Greenhow her life. And no city was

Above: The famous Confederate spy Rose O'Neale Greenhow drowned off the steamer Condor *while attempting to run the Union blockade at Wilmington in the early morning hours of October 1, 1864.*

COURTESY OF MARTIN PEEBLES.

Below: Captain John J. Hedrick led the Cape Fear Minutemen in an audacious capture of Fort Johnston at Smithville (present-day Southport) from its U.S. Army caretaker, Sergeant James Reilly, in the early morning hours of January 9, 1861.

COURTESY OF THE CAPE FEAR MUSEUM AND THE LOWER CAPE FEAR HISTORICAL SOCIETY.

more actively involved in blockade running during the Civil War than Wilmington, North Carolina. By the summer of 1863 Wilmington had emerged as the Confederacy's main seaport and by late the following year its most important city. At no other time did Wilmington play a more important role in the history of the United States than during the Civil War.

The contentious issue over the expansion of slavery finally tore the nation apart after decades of vitriolic debate and uneasy compromise. Beginning with South Carolina on December 20, 1860, Southern states carried out their threat to secede from the Union if Abraham Lincoln were elected president. Southerners did not trust Lincoln to defend their interests after he claimed that "this government cannot endure, permanently, half slave and half free." With Lincoln and the Republican Party set to take over the reigns of political power in early March 1861, Southerners believed that the federal government would not only attempt to halt the spread of slavery into the western territories, but go after the institution where it already existed. Shortly after the turn of the new year, six states followed South Carolina's lead in withdrawing from the Union, and together they created the Confederate States of America in February 1861, despite the efforts of most states to keep the nation together.

Upon seceding, South Carolinians confiscated federal property in the state, but were unsuccessful in taking Fort Sumter in Charleston harbor. While delegates negotiated with the federal government for the fort's peaceful transfer to state ownership, U.S. Army troops stationed in and around Charleston sought refuge in Sumter. Lame duck President James Buchanan attempted to relieve Fort Sumter's isolated garrison with reinforcements and supplies. On January 9, 1861, the steamship *Star of the West* attempted to enter Charleston's harbor but was driven off by a few well directed cannon shots from batteries onshore. The fate of the Union now hung in the balance at Charleston.

As the *Star of the West* approached Charleston, rumor spread through Wilmington that the federal government had also dispatched troops to reinforce the forts at the mouth of the Cape Fear River. In response, a group of militiamen from various Wilmington units calling themselves the Cape Fear Minutemen sailed downriver to take possession of the forts from their ordnance caretakers. Led by Captain John J. Hedrick, the militia seized Fort Johnston at Smithville from Sergeant James Reilly on January 9, 1861, and then, accompanied by the Smithville Guards, proceeded across the harbor the following day to capture Fort Caswell on Oak Island from Sergeant Frederick Dardingkiller.

When word of the captures reached Raleigh, Governor John W. Ellis sent instructions to Captain Hedrick to return the forts to their U.S. Army custodians. While the governor admired the audacity of the Cape Fear Minutemen, he also worried that the federal government might retaliate against the state, which was still in the Union. Hedrick and his men dutifully obeyed Ellis's orders, and then enjoyed a hero's welcome upon their return to Wilmington. The taking of Forts Johnston and Caswell by the Cape Fear Minutemen was the first public challenge to the federal government in North Carolina during the crisis of the Union, an act of defiance that conjured up memories of their ancestors' confrontation with the British royal governor, Governor William Tryon, during the Stamp Act trouble at Brunswick Town almost one hundred years earlier.

North Carolina moved closer to secession soon after the war began with the Battle of Fort Sumter, April 12-14, 1861. When President Lincoln requested troops from the states to put down the rebellion by military force, Governor Ellis adamantly declined, replying, "You can get no troops from North Carolina." The governor then ordered Colonel John L. Cantwell, a Wilmingtonian and commander of the Thirtieth North Carolina Militia, to retake Forts Johnston and Caswell "and hold them against all comers." On April 16, 1861, Cantwell and his men went downriver to recapture the forts, both of which remained in Southern hands until early 1865.

The newly created Confederate States of America was ill equipped to fight the Civil War. Since colonial days the South had largely been a region of planters, farmers, and slaves. Lacking the industrial capacity to meet its wartime needs, the Confederacy looked to Europe, especially Great Britain, to buy weapons, equipment, and provisions to support its war effort. To prevent trans-Atlantic trade from assisting the seceded states, President Lincoln proclaimed a naval blockade of the South on April 19, 1861. He expanded the blockade to include Virginia and North Carolina in a revised proclamation eight days later. The following month, on May 20, 1861, North Carolina joined the Southern Confederacy.

Declaring a blockade and making it effective were two different matters. The lack of U.S. Navy ships at the beginning of the war, the lengthy coastline from Virginia to Texas, and the large number of seaports and inlets to blockade made it virtually impossible to halt all waterborne commercial activity. Southern buyers and European suppliers soon established shipping firms to handle the overseas trade that ensued. The Anglo-Confederate Trading Company, William Crenshaw & Company, W. C. Bee Company, and other companies were soon doing all the business they could handle exchanging guns for cotton, and early on blockade running ships came and went almost at will. In high demand by the Confederate government were rifled muskets, artillery, ammunition, swords, bayonets, wool cloth for uniforms, blankets, shoes, medicines and food. Blockade running companies also imported civilian goods of all kinds—hoop skirts, parasols, kid gloves, and luxury items—on which they stood to make substantial profits through auctions. It proved to be a lucrative trade. The great risks shippers faced smuggling supplies through the blockade to satisfy the demand for items people found

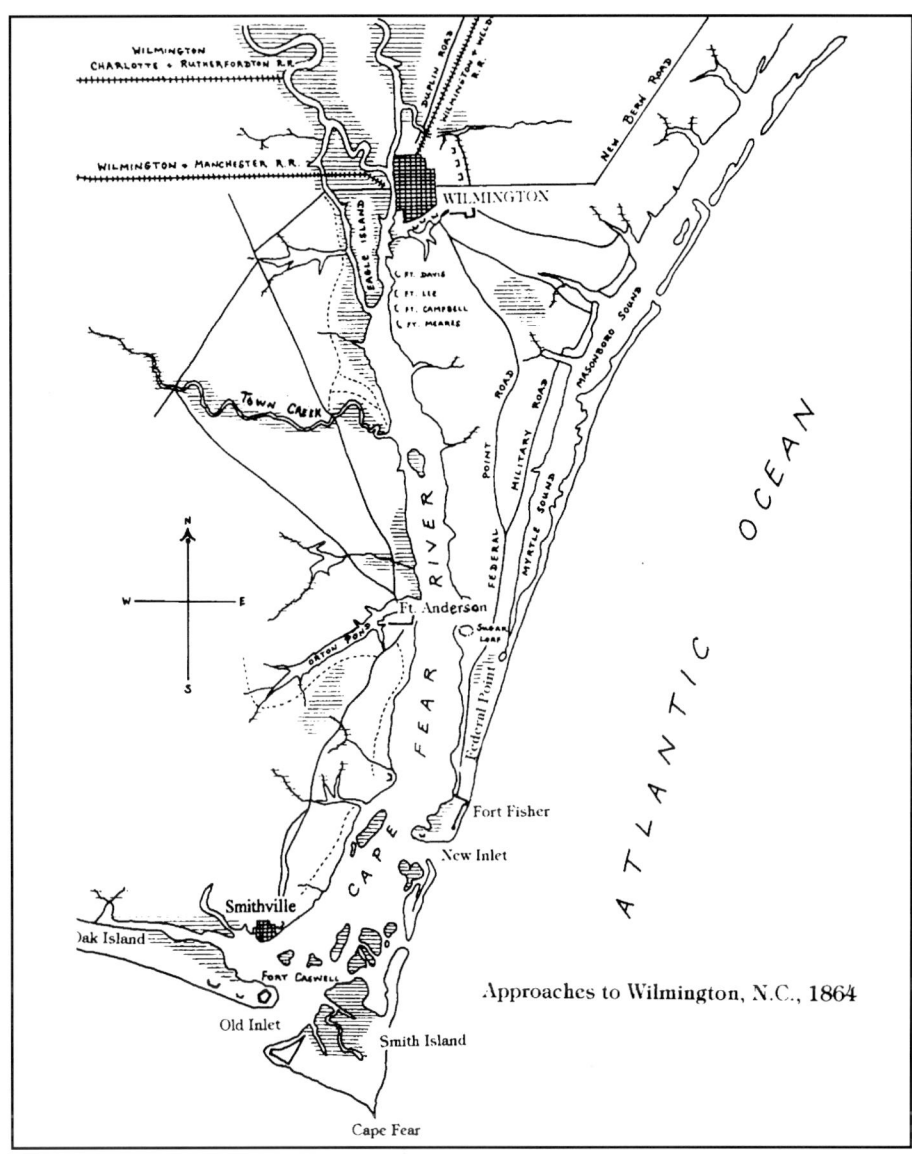

Approaches to Wilmington, N.C., 1864

✧

COURTESY OF CHRIS E. FONVIELLE, JR.

✧

Above: The blockade runner Advance, *owned and operated by North Carolina, made seventeen trips through the Union blockade before being captured near Wilmington in September 1864. Note the first national Confederate flag flying from her stern in this photograph taken while she was anchored at Nassau, New Providence, Bahamas, in 1863.*

COURTESY OF CHARLES V. PEERY.

Below: One of the most successful and popular Confederate sea captains was Wilmingtonian John Newland Maffitt, who commanded the commerce raider CSS Florida *early in the war and then the blockade runners* Florie *and* Owl.

COURTESY OF CHRIS E. FONVIELLE, JR.

difficult to procure elsewhere meant importers could charge whatever prices the market would bear, thus filling investors' pockets with cash. At the same time, the controversial business drove retail prices to levels most people could ill afford.

By 1865, more than sixteen hundred vessels of all classes—schooners, barks, and steamers foremost among them—had been employed as blockade runners. About thirteen hundred of them were sailing ships, used until 1863-1864 when the blockade had tightened to the extent that it became difficult to break the cordon of Union vessels by wind power alone. Steamships were used more often during the last year and a half of the war, employing both speed and stealth to challenge the blockade. About 70 different steamers with names like *Banshee*, *Hope*, *Phantom*, *Ranger*, and *Let Her Rip* operated in and out of Wilmington, enjoying a phenomenal success rate of about 85 percent.

Typical of this class of ship was the *Advance*. Built by Jones, Quiggin & Company in 1862 as the steam packet *Lord Clyde* in Greenock, Scotland, she was purchased by North Carolina for use as a blockade runner. The *Advance* made seventeen runs through the blockade before being captured by the USS *Santiago de Cuba* as she attempted to run out of Wilmington on September 10, 1864. The U.S. Navy subsequently purchased her from a prize court and converted her into the gunboat USS *Frolic* for blockading duty. The success of the *Advance* along with other blockade runners at Wilmington enabled North Carolina to feed, clothe, and equip its armed forces more effectively than any other Confederate state.

Wilmington offered great advantages for the commercial trade. The seaport was located near the neutral transshipment points of Bermuda and Nassau in the Bahamas, and, at twenty-eight miles from the mouth of the Cape Fear River, was far out of range of Union naval bombardment. Moreover, Wilmington had good lines of communication with the interior—the Cape Fear River and three railroads. The most important of the rail lines was the Wilmington & Weldon Railroad, the main supply route for General Robert E. Lee's Army of Northern Virginia.

Blockade running seaports like Wilmington attracted an odd mixture of humanity that transformed them into places almost unrecognizable from their pre-war days. The once quiet, relatively modest Tar Heel port town of almost ten thousand people in 1860 became an overcrowded, bawdy, and violent city. Captain John Wilkinson of the blockade runner *Robert E. Lee* recalled that the "staid old town of Wilmington was turned 'topsy-turvy' during the war. Here resorted the speculators from all parts of the South to attend the weekly auctions of imported cargoes; and the town was infested with rogues and desperadoes, who made a livelihood by robbery and murder. . .The civil authorities were powerless to prevent crime," Wilkinson recalled. "The agents and employees of the different blockade running companies, [however], lived in magnificent style." The profiteering and money-mongering in the blockade running trade lured crooks, confidence men, and prostitutes to Wilmington. Appalled by the appearance of unsavory characters and rising crime, many affluent residents left the city to refugee in safer locations on the sounds or upstate.

Blockade running led Wilmington to become a virtual ghost town in the autumn of 1862. Residents blamed the blockade runner *Kate* for inadvertently smuggling yellow fever into the city along with her cargo of supplies when she docked on August 6, 1862. Unfamiliar with the virus and its mosquito-borne transmission, physicians misdiagnosed the disease until it reached epidemic proportions in late September. As cases and fatalities mounted, citizens and military personnel evacuated Wilmington in droves, seeking havens closer to the ocean or in the interior of the state. Stores and businesses closed and boarded up and streets stood empty and silent except for the sounds of caregivers treading the walkways and death wagons rolling toward the cemeteries. By the time cold weather killed the disease at the end of November 1862, 1,500 cases of yellow fever had been reported in Wilmington alone and 654 Wilmingtonians were dead. Blockade running had indeed been death dealing.

The wartime upheaval in the Lower Cape Fear was mitigated, at least in part, by the contributions of women. As in most Southern and Northern cities and towns, the ladies of Wilmington formed philanthropic organizations to alleviate the sufferings of soldiers and their families. Mrs. Armand John DeRosset presided over the Soldiers' Aid Society (also known as the Ladies' Aid Society), that solicited donations from businesses and wealthy individuals to assist wounded or maimed soldiers returning from the battlefront and their needy wives and children on the home front. Bibles, blankets, quilts, sheets, towels, pillowcases, pants, socks, food, and money, of course, were always in high demand. Cape Fearians donated tens of thousands of dollars and tons of provisions and supplies to help the needy.

Not everyone was generous when called upon to donate, however, as Mary Ann Buie could attest. Miss Buie was well known in the Wilmington area as the "Soldier's Friend" because of her untiring efforts to provide for soldiers, especially those confined to hospitals. She beseeched blockade runners and blockade running companies for assistance because she knew that was where the money was. Most shipping firms and ships' officers and crewmen were gracious in giving, but William Crenshaw, who owned many fine blockade running ships, rebuffed Miss Buie's entreaties. Crenshaw's unmitigated greed eventually incurred Buie's wrath, as she told him that "she wished his next ship to enter would be lost." Within days of her curse being uttered, the Crenshaw steamer *Hebe* was run aground and destroyed near Fort Fisher on August 22, 1863. When Crenshaw remained steadfast in his refusal to subscribe to Buie's Soldiers' Relief Fund, she hexed him again. When all was said and done, Crenshaw had lost four ships, for which Miss Buie claimed credit.

Miss Buie's imprecations against William Crenshaw were recorded by James Ryder Randall, an agent with the W. C. Bee Company, because they were so unusual and she was so eccentric. Most ladies, however, practiced more conventional means of helping soldiers—collecting donations, meeting trains at the depots to hand out fried chicken, ham biscuits, and lemonade, writing letters to their loved ones, offering goods and provisions or simply words of encouragement and appreciation. Their support to the Confederate war effort was incalculable.

Thousands of young men from Wilmington and surrounding towns and counties enlisted in the Confederate army for the war. Many of them were members of pre-war militia units like the Wilmington Light Infantry, the German Volunteers, and the Cape Fear Riflemen, that were assigned to state regiments. The Cape Fear Riflemen became Company F, Third Regiment North Carolina State Troops while the German Volunteers, which required German heritage for entry into the unit, became Company A and the Wilmington Light Infantry became Company G of Eighteenth Regiment North Carolina State Troops. In fact, eight of the ten companies that comprised the Eighteenth North Carolina Troops came from the Cape Fear area. By 1863, Colonel John D. Barry of Wilmington had become the regiment's commanding officer.

While many Cape Fear boys went off to fight mostly in Virginia, hundreds of others remained in their home region to build and man

✧

Above: Captain Michael P. Usina of the blockade runner Rattlesnake *was known as "the man who owned the dog," a terrier named Tinker who led a charmed life and brought good luck to his master's maritime exploits.*

COURTESY OF CHARLES V. PEERY.

Below: The Confederate Grays of Duplin County, North Carolina, trained at Smithville (present-day Southport) in early 1862 before heading off to war in Virginia as Company E, Twentieth Regiment North Carolina Troops.

COURTESY OF THE NORTH CAROLINA STATE ARCHIVES.

✧

Above: Confederate Fort Anderson, built atop the ruins of Brunswick Town, was the strongest interior work guarding Wilmington and the Cape Fear River during the Civil War.
COURTESY OF CHRIS E. FONVIELLE, JR.

Middle: An unflattering sketch of philanthropist Mary Ann Buie, who was known for her untiring efforts and sometimes aggressive tactics in raising money for her Confederate Soldiers' Relief Fund.
COURTESY OF THE LOWER CAPE FEAR HISTORICAL SOCIETY.

Below: Colonel John D. Barry, Wilmington-born commander of the Eighteenth Regiment North Carolina Troops, whose orders led his soldiers to accidentally shoot the famed Confederate General Thomas J. "Stonewall" Jackson at the Battle of Chancellorsville, Virginia, on the night of May 2, 1863. COURTESY OF CHRIS E. FONVIELLE, JR.

fortifications to protect Wilmington, which increasingly became an important seaport. Mostly Tar Heel units garrisoned the forts and batteries in and around the town, but regiments from other states in the Confederacy came and went as circumstances dictated their need for defensive purposes. Wilmington essentially became an armed camp as thousands of soldiers, sailors, and marines garrisoned the area.

Confederate engineers designed a vast network of forts and batteries in the lower Cape Fear to defend the inlets that blockade runners used to enter the harbor, the city where blockade runners unloaded their valuable cargoes, and the railroads along which arms, equipment, and supplies were sent to soldiers on the battlefront and provisions to civilians on the home front. Next to Charleston, Wilmington was the most heavily fortified place on the Atlantic seaboard. The town itself was surrounded by strong defenses while additional batteries were scattered up and down the river and along the beaches. The strongest interior work was Fort Anderson, constructed beginning in late March 1862 atop the ruins of Brunswick Town. It guarded the river channel just abreast of the site as well as the western land approaches to Wilmington.

The largest and best armed forts were built to safeguard the river entrances for blockade runners. Large seacoast cannon in Forts Caswell and Campbell and Battery Shaw on Oak Island and Fort Holmes on Bald Head Island overlooked Old Inlet, while Fort Fisher on Federal Point (called Confederate Point by Southerners during the war) guarded New Inlet at the southern tip of New Hanover County. Colonel William Lamb of the Thirty-sixth North Carolina Troops was largely responsible for designing and building mighty Fort Fisher, which was considered so strong that engineers on both sides considered it impregnable, calling it the "Gibraltar of the South." New Inlet soon became the most popular passageway into the harbor for blockade runners because of the protection Fort Fisher's guns provided. The fort's garrison and Union blockaders dueled on a regular basis for control of the waters off New Inlet, and for most of the war the Confederates prevailed. But the Cape Fear District commander, Major General W. H. C. Whiting, knew that sooner or later a Union attack against his forts was coming.

So important was the Confederate lifeline through Wilmington that as early as January 1863, General Robert E. Lee cautioned that the seaport "must be defended at all hazards." By 1864 Lee's message took on a greater sense of urgency. "If Wilmington falls I cannot maintain my army," Lee predicted. The message was clear: the survival of Lee's Army of Northern Virginia and thus the Confederacy depended upon the survival of Wilmington as a blockade running seaport.

The U.S. Navy also understood Wilmington's importance, as its sailors watched blockade runners coming and going on an almost daily basis. Seemingly powerless to stop the trade, however, the navy needed the assistance of an expeditionary force to capture the forts at the mouth of the Cape Fear River and close Wilmington to blockade running. For most of the war, however, the Lincoln administration and the U.S. War Department took little interest in Wilmington, more concerned as they were with capturing Richmond and other strategic cities like Vicksburg, Mississippi; Chattanooga, Tennessee; and Atlanta, Georgia. Of the Confederate seaports still open to overseas trade,

only Charleston, where the war had begun, attracted intense popular and political interest. Not until the late summer of 1864 was U.S. Secretary of the Navy Gideon Welles able to convince President Lincoln and General U. S. Grant to support a combined army-navy attack against Wilmington, by then the last major seaport open to trade with the outside world.

Fort Fisher became the principal target. Because it guarded the northernmost passageway into the Cape Fear River, capturing it would seal both inlets to the illicit trade. Wilmington-bound blockade runners entering through Old Inlet could not get upriver past Fort Fisher if Union forces held Federal Point. Moreover, the U.S. Navy, which would lead the attack, hoped a great victory against the Confederacy's strongest fort guarding the South's last major seaport, would gain them some much desired publicity. Throughout the war, the navy believed that the U.S. Army was extolled for its role in combined operations while the U.S. Navy was neglected.

U.S. Navy and Army forces attacked Fort Fisher twice before capturing the stronghold. The first assault came at Christmas 1864. For two days a naval task force of sixty-four warships, the largest fleet assembled during the war and commanded by Rear Admiral David D. Porter, unleashed the greatest naval bombardment of the Civil War. Despite the severity of the shelling, however, the 20,271 iron projectiles thrown at the fort did not soften the defenses enough to warrant a ground assault by 6,500 army troops, prompting their commander, Major General Benjamin F. Butler, to abort the mission. Colonel Lamb and General Whiting inside the fort were jubilant over the garrison's successful defense.

A firestorm of controversy erupted in the North over the failure at Fort Fisher. General Grant replaced the discredited Benjamin Butler with a new army commander, Brigadier General Alfred H. Terry, and requested Admiral Porter to renew the attack as soon as possible. Porter's fleet accompanied by army transports bearing an increased force of ninety-six hundred troops, returned to Fort Fisher on the night of January 12, 1865. Colonel Lamb had anticipated a quick return of the Union fleet and made the necessary repairs to his hard hit fort, but Confederate headquarters in Wilmington was totally unprepared. General Braxton Bragg, who had been sent from Richmond to assume command from General Whiting because of Whiting's harsh criticism of President Jefferson Davis, had kept much needed reinforcements close to Wilmington, some twenty miles from Fort Fisher. By the time Bragg's soldiers arrived in the vicinity of Fisher early the following morning, January 13, Union troops had already come ashore and were making preparations to attack the fort.

For two and one half days, January 13-15, 1865, Admiral Porter's fleet poured another massive number of shot and shell—19,682—into Fort Fisher. This time the fire was much more accurate, dismounting or destroying much of the fort's artillery and making the defenses more vulnerable to a ground assault. Union army troops, assisted by a column of volunteer sailors and marines from various ships in the task force, charged Fort Fisher late on the afternoon of January 15. Confederate soldiers, including Colonel Lamb and General Whiting, came out of their underground bombproofs to

✧

Top, left: Major General W. H. C. Whiting commanded the District of the Cape Fear for much of the war, planning and supervising the construction of defenses for Wilmington's protection, including mighty Fort Fisher, the Confederacy's strongest seacoast fortification.

COURTESY OF THE LIBRARY OF CONGRESS.

Above: U.S. Navy Lieutenant William B. Cushing with the North Atlantic Blockading Squadron off Wilmington struck fear in the hearts of his Confederate antagonists when he staged several daring commando-like raids behind enemy lines at the Lower Cape Fear in 1864.

COURTESY OF PETER TUITE.

Below: Fort Fisher's most famous piece of ordnance was this British-manufactured 8-inch, 150-pounder Armstrong rifled cannon, brought into Wilmington on board the blockade runner Hope in late August or early September 1864. The U.S. Army took it as a trophy of war when Fort Fisher fell in 1865 and subsequently placed it at the U.S. Military Academy, West Point, New York.

COURTESY OF THE LIBRARY OF CONGRESS.

CHAPTER VI

✧

Above: Colonel William Lamb, Confederate commander of Fort Fisher, and his wife "Daisy" lived with two of their young children in this small clapboard cottage built by his soldiers about one half mile north of the fort on Confederate Point. Daisy and the children's presence allowed Lamb to maintain a semblance of normalcy in the whirlwind of war.

COURTESY OF THE FORT FISHER STATE HISTORIC SITE.

Below: U.S. Rear Admiral David D. Porter commanded the largest naval task force assembled during the Civil War to attack Fort Fisher with the two largest bombardments of the war, at Christmas 1864 and in mid-January 1865.

COURTESY OF LIBRARY OF CONGRESS.

defend the fort, but they were vastly outnumbered and overwhelmed. After hours of hand-to-hand combat, Confederate forces surrendered Fort Fisher to General Terry's men.

With Fort Fisher now in Federal hands, Wilmington was no longer open to blockade running. Acting on General Bragg's instructions, the Confederates abandoned the forts at Old Inlet and retreated up the Cape Fear River to take up new lines of defense at Fort Anderson at Brunswick Point and Sugar Loaf hill on the east bank of the river. Bragg established his field headquarters at Sugar Loaf. In mid-February, Union forces advanced upriver to attack Wilmington. Confederate troops fought a series of delaying actions at Town Creek in Brunswick County and at Forks Road three miles below Wilmington, but were eventually forced to abandon the city. The Confederates retreated northward to join other armies in the interior of the state, while Union forces occupied Wilmington on February 22, 1865. As Robert E. Lee had predicted if his lifeline through Wilmington was severed, he could no longer maintain his army in Virginia. He evacuated his position near Petersburg in early April but was run down and forced to surrender to General Grant at Appomattox Courthouse on April 9, 1865. In retrospect, the outcome of the war had probably been determined by the time Major General William T. Sherman captured Atlanta in early September 1864, but the fall of Wilmington the following winter certainly hastened the downfall of the Confederacy. By 1863 Wilmington had become the Confederacy's most valuable seaport. By late 1864, Wilmington had become the Confederacy's most important city. By the spring of 1865, Wilmington was occupied by Union forces.

Defeat came hard for Wilmingtonians, in part because of the destruction the town suffered during the fighting, but also because of the significant social change that came about with the destruction of slavery. But the war also brought about a great economic boon for Wilmington, as local shippers and merchants took advantage of blockade running trade relations they had established during the war to deal in even larger amounts of cotton and other exports directly to Europe in the postwar years. As fate would have it, the Civil War catapulted Wilmington from a regional port into an international seaport.

CHAPTER VII

THE AFRICAN AMERICAN EXPERIENCE

Africans and African Americans were among the earliest settlers of the Lower Cape Fear. Their names and stories may have been lost to time, but not their contributions to colonization and development of the area. The Adventurers and Planters of Cape Feare, led by John Vassall, brought their African slaves with them from Barbados to settle Charles Towne in 1664. The profit-minded Lords Proprietors paved the way for slavery in the region by offering the English settlers additional land for every Negro they brought to the colony. The Moore family and their supporters immigrated to the Lower Cape Fear beginning in 1726, bringing with them slaves from the rice fields of South Carolina and the tobacco fields of Albemarle County, North Carolina.

The African American population grew as demand increased for laborers to work the fields, forests, and river. Slaves comprised the principal workforces for the cultivation of rice and indigo, boxing of pine trees for turpentine, cutting of hard wood trees for lumber, and loading and unloading ships. By the mid-1700s more than half of all white households in New Hanover County owned slaves, with most ownership concentrated in the hands of elite planters. Indeed, 73 percent of Cape Fear slaves in 1770 were possessed by masters with 20 or more slaves. King Roger Moore of Orton Plantation owned 250 bondservants at the time of his death in 1751. White Cape Fearians depended heavily upon slaves for much of the labor that supported their individual wealth and the economic development of the region.

By the mid-1700s, slavery was firmly entrenched in the Lower Cape Fear. The growing number of slaves, however, raised concerns among whites of slave revolts, particularly in the wake of the 1739 Stono Rebellion in South Carolina, the largest slave uprising in colonial America. To ensure the safety of white people and obedience of black laborers, North Carolina's General Assembly began passing laws for the colony and approving town laws known as the slave code that regulated the activities and behavior of slaves. As early as 1745, Wilmington commissioners sought to monitor slaves in local markets where they sold, bartered, and negotiated deals largely independent of their masters. Excessive privileges for those in bondage would not be tolerated. In the coming years, additional laws established curfews for slaves, required them to carry identification, limited

✧

Scottish-born artist John M. Falconer sketched "Negro Huts in Wilmington" on his visit to the Carolina port town about 1880.
COURTESY OF CHRIS E. FONVIELLE, JR.

Above: Unidentified African American friends photographed by Charles W. Yates, Wilmington, N.C., about 1875.
COURTESY OF THE NEW HANOVER COUNTY PUBLIC LIBRARY.

Top, right: Many African Americans worked the pine barrens of southeastern North Carolina, boxing pine trees for crude turpentine in the naval stores industry.
COURTESY OF THE LOWER CAPE FEAR HISTORICAL SOCIETY.

Right: Title page of the revised edition of Walker's *Appeal to the Coloured Citizens of the World, a controversial anti-slavery treatise first published in Boston in 1829 by David Walker, a Wilmington-born free black.*
COURTESY OF THE NEW HANOVER COUNTY PUBLIC LIBRARY.

their mobility, and prohibited them from assembling in large numbers and fraternizing with free blacks.

Extant records reveal no major slave rebellions in the Lower Cape Fear but growing evidence suggests that a plot was uncovered in 1753, and resulted in the execution of the conspirators. Allegedly, their decapitated heads were stuck on poles along a thoroughfare leading into town that became known as Negro Head Road in the area of today's Highway 421 North as a warning to other potential insurrectionists.

Given the restrictions under which slaves lived and labored, it was little wonder that they took advantage of any opportunity to escape to freedom. At least 36 slaves, including 12 women, fled on March 3, 1776, to British forces in the Cape Fear estuary. Soon thereafter, fifteen more slaves absconded from their masters and subsequently joined the British Royal Navy. Increasingly, the Cape Fear River became a conduit for slave escapes.

Both slavery and the slave code expanded in the South between 1800 and 1861. The

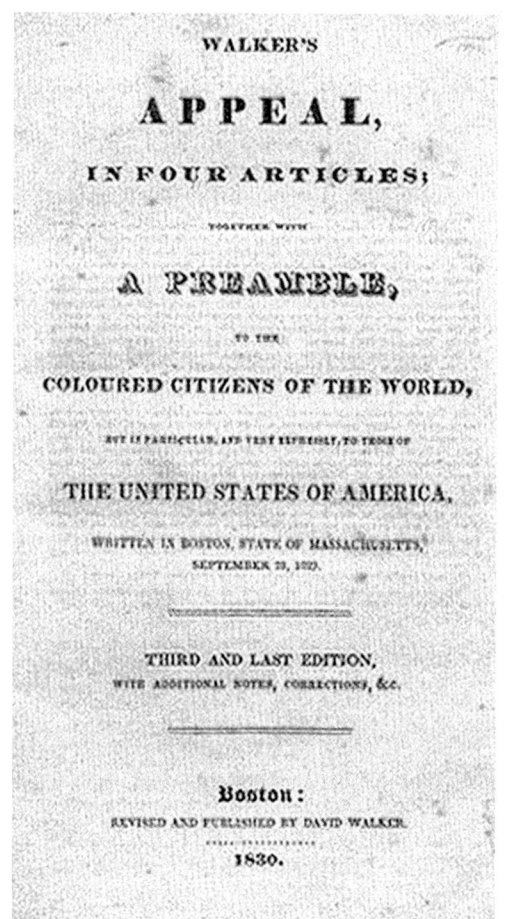

introduction of the cotton gin in 1793 had greatly improved production and heightened demand for the high grade Southern fiber. The growth of the Cotton Kingdom increased the need for additional slaves, especially in the cotton belt of the Deep South, but also in the port towns, where cotton was exported to the North and to Europe. Slaves comprised much of the workforce along the docks and wharves in Wilmington and other Southern seaports.

The swelling slave population in the antebellum period, as in colonial days, fueled white fears of slave resistance. Those concerns were exacerbated by the publication of *Appeal to the Coloured Citizens*, a controversial piece of anti-slavery literature that advocated the overthrow of slavery by violence. Printed in Boston, Massachusetts in 1829, the pamphlet's author was David Walker, a free black from Wilmington, North Carolina. Born about 1796, Walker was the son of a free black mother, which determined his status. But Walker's father was a slave, bonded to a cruel system that Walker grew to hate, provoking him to leave the South. After settling in Boston, Walker became the agent for *Freedom's Journal*, an African American anti-slavery newspaper published in New York City, and a leader in the burgeoning abolitionist movement. Walker's

Appeal saw wide distribution in the North but had to be smuggled into the South where anti-slavery treatises were banned.

Raising far greater concern among whites than Walker's inflammatory publication, however, was Nat Turner's slave revolt in Southampton County, Virginia, in August 1831. About sixty white people were murdered by Turner's insurrectionists, as well as an untold number of blacks by white vigilantes. In response to Turner's rebellion, the North Carolina legislature passed additional laws in the 1830s to tighten the state's grip on African Americans. New regulations forbade whites from teaching slaves to read and write, and restricted conditions under which masters could free their slaves. Even free blacks were slowly but surely stripped of their civil liberties. No longer could they vote in state elections, possess firearms without a license, or preach in public. By 1861, free blacks were also banned from owning or controlling slave property, making it impossible for them to purchase freedom for a wife, husband or child.

Slavery and race relations had always been complex issues in the South. The patriarchal system required masters to provide care and protection for their slaves. To be sure, white owners exploited their slaves for labor and profit, but they also referred to them as extended family members. Some slaves were even allowed guarded entry into white society. Omar Ibn Said, a member of the Fula tribe of Senegal, West Africa, was sold into slavery in 1807, eventually becoming the property of the prominent James Owen family of Bladen County, North Carolina. A devout Muslim, Said also practiced Christianity in his later years, worshipping at the all-white First Presbyterian Church in Wilmington, where he moved with his master in 1836. Said apparently was accorded considerable respect and freedom to move about Wilmington's white dominated world, unlike the vast majority of slaves who were largely viewed with suspicion and mistrust.

Even though slaves were restrained, this was also a world in which free blacks, at least prior to the Civil War, could and did acquire property and accumulate wealth. James D. Sampson, a noted mulatto contractor in antebellum Wilmington, had owned as many as 25 slaves, $26,000 in real estate and $10,000 in personal property at the time of his death about 1863. Sampson's children were beneficiaries of their father's wealth, with many of them being educated in Northern colleges and enjoying successful professional careers. One of his daughters, Susan, taught school in Washington, D.C., and later married James B. Dudley, principal of Wilmington's Peabody School and editor of the *Wilmington Chronicle* in the 1880s.

The Civil War profoundly altered race relations and demographics in Wilmington and the Lower Cape Fear. African Americans were both an asset and a liability to the South's war effort. They continued to perform much of the

❖

Above: Omar Ibn Said, a member of the Fula tribe of Senegal, West Africa who later became a slave of the James Owen family of Bladen County, was affectionately known as Uncle Moreau when he lived in Wilmington from 1836 until about 1860.
COURTESY OF THE NEW HANOVER COUNTY PUBLIC LIBRARY.

Below: A scarce Civil War period bill of sale for three slaves—Tom, Mona, and child Musses—purchased for $365 by John T. Hewett of Wilmington.
COURTESY OF CHRIS E. FONVIELLE, JR.

CHAPTER VII

✧

Above: William B. Gould escaped slavery in Wilmington on the night of September 21, 1862, when he and seven fellow slaves rowed a boat to the mouth of the Cape Fear River, where they were rescued by the blockader USS Cambridge *early the following morning.*

COURTESY OF WILLIAM B. GOULD IV.

Below: Black soldiers in blue of Company E, Fourth United States Colored Troops participated in the Battles of Fort Fisher and the Wilmington Campaign, 1864-1865.

COURTESY OF THE LIBRARY OF CONGRESS.

hard labor, albeit compulsory, that supported the Confederacy—cultivating the cotton that was exported to Europe in exchange for much-needed supplies, constructing fortifications to defend the Cape Fear, and working in the shipyards, on the railroads and the docks and wharves. Black workers on the home front also left white men free to fight on the battlefront.

While blacks may have openly donned masks of devotion for the benefit of their masters, behind the scenes many of them attempted to undermine the Confederate cause, the cornerstone of which was the belief that African Americans were inferior and that the South was a white man's country. Abraham Galloway, who was born a slave in Brunswick County, emerged as the leader of the black insurgency movement in North Carolina during the Civil War. He had escaped slavery in 1857, stowing away on a schooner in Wilmington bound for Philadelphia. Soon after the war broke out, Galloway returned to North Carolina to serve as a Union spy and recruiter of United States Colored Troops. At war's end, Galloway moved back to Wilmington, where he became active in political affairs. In 1868 he was elected to the North Carolina legislature, serving as a Republican senator from New Hanover County until his untimely death two years later.

Like Galloway, who initiated his role as an activist by escaping slavery, many bonded persons sought to free themselves from their dreaded imprisonment. Perhaps the most noted escape from the Lower Cape Fear during the Civil War occurred when William B. Gould and seven other slaves fled Wilmington in late September 1862. At the time, Wilmington was gripped by a devastating yellow fever epidemic, prompting many white residents and military personnel to leave the town for safer havens in the interior of the state, along the sounds, or at Smithville near the mouth of the river. The evacuation of the town provided a golden opportunity for slaves to escape. Gould, a skilled artisan whose owner, Nicholas Nixon, hired him out to work in Wilmington homes like the Bellamy Mansion, made his getaway with fellow slaves on the night of September 21, 1862. With the lack of security forces in town, Gould and his cohorts were able to confiscate a boat and launch it at the foot of Orange Street. They furiously rowed twenty-eight miles down the Cape Fear River in a single night without being detected. Early the next morning the USS *Cambridge* rescued them off Old Inlet. Upon gaining his freedom, Gould joined the U.S. Navy, serving briefly with the Wilmington Blockading Squadron. Other slaves fled to freedom at about the same time, making Gould's flight part of a great escape.

Slave escapes were a constant problem for Confederate authorities. African Americans knew that freedom was as close as Union blockading ships deployed just offshore and fled to them when opportunities presented themselves. While Gould joined the U.S. Navy, other escapees enlisted in the U.S. Army. Former slaves from the Lower Cape Fear fought with regiments of United States Colored Troops in the Battles of Fort Fisher and the Wilmington Campaign in the last winter of the war. When victorious Union troops paraded into

Wilmington on February 22, 1865, an unidentified black woman recognized her son whom she had not seen since he had escaped slavery. Now he was returning home a black soldier in blue and a free man. She ran out into the street to embrace him as his unit marched past, and together they cried. She, like her son, was now also free.

As the war slowly ground to a halt, thousands of African Americans migrated to Wilmington. Most of them were escaped slaves who had attached themselves to Union General William T. Sherman's army as it marched through the Carolinas in 1865. Their numbers grew so rapidly that they soon became a burden to Sherman's military operations. Consequently, as soon as his army reached Fayetteville, North Carolina, the general disposed of them by sending them down the Cape Fear River to Wilmington.

The first of the refugees arrived in the port town by the middle of March 1865, followed soon thereafter by a large column of about six thousand people. Many more arrived in the coming days so that by early April, 8,000 to 10,000 displaced African Americans thronged the streets of Wilmington. In great need of sustenance and shelter, they presented a problem for the U.S. Army's Commissary Department, which did not have enough supplies to feed and clothe them.

✧

Top, left: Abraham Galloway, the son of a slave woman and, reputedly, a prominent Brunswick County white man named John W. Galloway, served as a spy for the Union army in North Carolina during the Civil War and represented New Hanover County as a Republican state senator from 1868 until his untimely death in 1870.
COURTESY OF THE NEW HANOVER COUNTY PUBLIC LIBRARY.

Top, right: A scarce mid-nineteenth century ambrotype of an African American identified as "Jordan Loftin, Wilmington, N. C." dressed in what appears to be a fireman's uniform.
COURTESY OF MARY ANN POWELL.

Left: Carte de visite photographs of Wilmington-born James B. Dudley and his wife Susan Sampson Dudley about 1880. Dudley served as principal of Wilmington's Peabody School and edited the Wilmington Chronicle, *while his wife was both a mother and a playwright.*
COURTESY OF THE NEW HANOVER COUNTY PUBLIC LIBRARY.

CHAPTER VII

Above: An unidentified African American mason of Giblem Lodge, Wilmington's oldest black Masonic institution, dressed in his regalia in this Henry Cronenburg photograph from about 1885.

COURTESY OF CHRIS E. FONVIELLE, JR.

Right: Alex Manly, mulatto editor and publisher of the African American Wilmington Daily Record, *lost his printing press and offices when Love & Charity Hall was burned by a rampageous mob of white supremacists on the morning of November 10, 1898.*

COURTESY OF THE NEW HANOVER COUNTY PUBLIC LIBRARY.

Military authorities and civilians alike tried to alleviate the refugees' suffering. Residents took some of them into their homes, while the army temporarily placed others onto abandoned farms and plantations or into vacant Confederate forts in the Cape Fear. Many refugees were eventually transferred to the Sea Islands off South Carolina and Georgia, but hundreds of others, including veterans of the U.S. Colored Troops, made Wilmington their home. By 1870, African Americans comprised 59 percent of Wilmington's population and 52 percent of New Hanover County's population. In fact, blacks remained in the majority in both the city and county until after the turn of the twentieth century.

Wilmington became a Mecca for African Americans in the late nineteenth century. The changing economic and political climate led the city to become known as one of the best places for blacks in the South. African Americans figured prominently in Wilmington's business life. They became lawyers, bankers, brokers, grocers, druggists, craftsmen, journalists, barbers, shoemakers, and tradesmen. John C. Dancy served as collector of customs for the Port of Wilmington in the late 1890s. Thomas C. Miller was a real estate agent and auctioneer in the city. Alex and Frank Manly owned and published the *Wilmington Daily Record*, purportedly the only daily African American newspaper in the nation at the time. Frederick Cutlar Sadgwar was a master builder and civic leader. African Americans also gained considerable political power in Wilmington. While "Negro domination" never occurred, as white critics charged, black Republicans comprised a substantial voting bloc and held important positions as city aldermen, magistrates, and justices of the peace.

A black majority, economic competition, growing black political power, reports of black related crime, and deep-seated racism intensified anxiety in Wilmington's white community that led to violence in early November 1898. The North Carolina Democratic Party waged a white supremacy campaign that summer and autumn to drive Republicans and their allies, known collectively as Fusionists, out of state and local offices. White fear tactics and intimidation kept many African Americans from voting on November 9, ensuring victory for the Democrats. Resentful whites also determined to retaliate against Alex Manly who had written a controversial editorial defending black men of alleged crimes of rape in the South that appeared in the *Wilmington Daily Record* before the November elections.

Democratic newspapers reprinted incendiary distortions of Manly's editorial to inflame white anger that erupted in violence on the morning of November 10, 1898. A rampageous mob stormed the offices of the *Wilmington Daily Record* at Love and Charity Hall on South Seventh Street in Wilmington, destroying the printing press and burning the building. The

audacious incident provoked a race riot in Wilmington that resulted in the death of an unknown number of black citizens, the wounding of some whites, and destruction of property, especially on the north side of the city. White conspirators used the violence as an excuse to seize control of the local government before the traditional peaceful transfer of power was allowed to occur, and to exile prominent black politicians and businessmen and their white allies from the city. Alex Manly and his family fled to Philadelphia and never returned to Wilmington. The Wilmington Race Riot of 1898 was the only political coup d'etat in U.S. history and, sadly, set the tone for uneasy race relations in the community for the next seventy-five years.

The considerable economic and political progress made by African Americans in Wilmington in the decades after the Civil War suffered a terrible setback as a result of the Riot of 1898. Perhaps the saving grace for the black community was the creation of a fine educational tradition in Williston High School. Funded by Samuel Williston, a Northern philanthropist, the school began as Williston Graded School. In 1916, it became Williston Industrial School, to be replaced seven years later by Williston High School, the first accredited high school in the state for African American students. Williston soon gained a reputation as one of the finest public educational institutions in the country, producing many well educated and talented young people who believed that, despite the racism they faced in their own community and the nation at large, they could make a difference. A sampling of Williston graduates reads like a who's who of African Americans: Frederick C. Alston, Jr., nationally known artist; John R. Larkins, North Carolina Commissioner of Public Welfare and author of books on black social issues; Meadowlark Lemon, the "Clown Prince" of the Harlem Globetrotters professional basketball team; Sam Bowens, major league baseball player with the Baltimore Orioles and Washington Senators; and Althea Gibson, the first black woman to win international tennis championships at Wimbleton.

Through the years, the Cape Fear produced many other outstanding African American leaders and notables: James K. Cutlar, North Carolina State Inspector of Naval Stores and political activist in the 1870s; James B. Dudley, educator and newspaper editor in the 1880s; Minnie Evans, internationally known twentieth century folk artist whose works have been exhibited in Wilmington, New York and London; Alfred A. Howe, master builder in Wilmington; Caterina Jarboro, world famous opera singer in the 1930s; Thomas H. Jones, former slave and ordained minister of North

✧

Above: The beautiful Caterina Jarboro of Wilmington became a world renowned opera singer by the 1930s, performing in Italy, France, Austria, and at Thalian Hall in her hometown.
COURTESY OF THE NEW HANOVER COUNTY PUBLIC LIBRARY.

Below: Dr. Hubert A. Eaton, a physician and leading civil rights leader, worked tirelessly and patiently to integrate Wilmington's public schools, hospitals, and other institutions in the 1950s and 1960s.
COURTESY OF THE NEW HANOVER COUNTY PUBLIC LIBRARY.

Carolina's A. M. E. Church; Michael Jordan, arguably the greatest player in the history of the National Basketball Association; George W. Price, Jr., craftsman and North Carolina Republican representative, 1860s-1880s; Armand W. Scott, lawyer and political activist in the late nineteenth century; Herbert Bell Shaw, pastor of St. Luke's Methodist Church in Wilmington and later bishop of the diocese; John E. Taylor, the first black man to be appointed deputy collector of customs for the Port of Wilmington, a position he held for twenty-five years in the late 1800s; and Robert R. Taylor, graduate of Massachusetts Institute of Technology in 1892, and the first professionally trained African American architect in the United States.

Special note should be made of Dr. Hubert A. Eaton, Sr., leader of the civil rights movement in Wilmington in the 1950s-1960s. Dr. Eaton was born in Fayetteville, North Carolina, but grew up in tidewater Virginia. His connection to Wilmington was through his Wilmington-born wife, Celeste Burnett. A graduate of the University of Michigan School of Medicine, Dr. Eaton moved to the Tar Heel port city in 1943 to practice medicine with his father-in-law. Eaton became chief of staff at Wilmington's all-black Community Hospital, president of the Old North State Medical Society, and eventually a member of UNC Wilmington's Board of Trustees. He was also a champion tennis player in his younger years and trained Althea Gibson at his home tennis court on Orange Street in Wilmington. Despite all of his other great accomplishments, it was as a civil rights activist that Dr. Eaton made his mark on Wilmington. He tirelessly and patiently used the legal system to desegregate New Hanover County schools, James Walker Memorial Hospital, Wilmington Public Library, Wilmington Municipal Golf Course, and the YMCA. He later chronicled his struggles and successes in his autobiography, *Every Man Should Try*. Dr. Hubert A. Eaton, the Martin Luther King, Jr., of southeastern North Carolina, passed away on September 4, 1991.

Dr. Eaton's achievements notwithstanding, hard days of tense race relations were still ahead for Wilmington. The forced closing of the all-black Williston High School by the New Hanover Board of Education and the assassination of Martin Luther King, Jr. in 1968

✧

Michael Jordan of Wilmington, wearing the now famous number 23 jersey, attempted to drive past an opponent in a 1981 Laney High School basketball game, as photographed by Dan Sears. Jordan went on to stardom with the University of North Carolina Tar Heels in the Atlantic Coast Conference and the Chicago Bulls of the National Basketball Association.

COURTESY OF THE NEW HANOVER COUNTY PUBLIC LIBRARY.

provoked racial unrest in the city that lasted several years. Through it all, bad memories of the Wilmington Race Riot of 1898 haunted the city's black community.

Great efforts to improve race relations in Wilmington, however, are currently underway. One hundred years after the Wilmington Race Riot, a Centennial Foundation was created to study the history of race in the city and to recommend ways to better conditions. In 1998, UNC Wilmington hosted a symposium featuring noted scholars who addressed the historical issues surrounding the riot. More recently, the North Carolina Office of Archives and History, working with the 1898 Wilmington Race Riot Commission, published an extensive report on the racial episode and made recommendations for righting past injustices. Plans have also been made to erect a memorial to the victims of the riot in historic downtown Wilmington. These endeavors have prompted Wilmingtonians to confront their difficult past and to seek new ways to bring all of the city's residents together, regardless of race, and to create a more equitable society. From slavery to freedom, African Americans, then as now, are making Wilmington and the Lower Cape Fear a better place to live.

CHAPTER VIII

THE GREATEST GENERATION OF CAPE FEARIANS

Chris E. "Gene" Fonvielle and Daniel D. Cameron could never have imagined what life had in store for them when they departed Wilmington for the Virginia Military Institute in Lexington in the late summer of 1938. Friends since their days at New Hanover High School, they determined to attend the same college and room together. The nation was at war with both Germany and Japan when Fonvielle and Cameron were graduated four years later. Commissioned second lieutenants in the U.S. Army, they were soon off to boot camp and then to Europe to fight the Nazis. Lieutenant Fonvielle served as a forward observer with the Seventh Armored Division while Lieutenant Cameron (later commissioned as a captain) fought with the 430th AAA Battalion. The war would forever change them and their hometown.

Only during the Civil War did Wilmington and the Lower Cape Fear play such an important role in the history of the United States as in World War II. Thousands of young Cape Fear men and women served their country in both the European and Pacific theaters, and 191 soldiers from New Hanover County alone did not return. Two New Hanover High School graduates—Lieutenant Charles P. Murray (class of 1938) and U.S. Navy Corpsman William D. "Billy" Halyburton, Jr. (class of 1943, killed in action on Okinawa, May 10, 1945)—received the nation's highest military award, the Congressional Medal of Honor, for valor in combat. People who remained on the home front also contributed to the war effort as the nation mobilized as it never had before to meet a foreign enemy.

The greatest wartime enterprise in Wilmington centered on shipbuilding. With the federal government's increased need for merchant and cargo vessels, the Newport News Shipbuilding Company of Virginia established the North Carolina Shipbuilding Company in Wilmington as a subsidiary firm in early 1941. The shipbuilding industry in Wilmington was as old as the city itself, but had never witnessed the level of activity that ensued during World War II. The North Carolina Shipbuilding Company became the state's largest employer with 23,000 people, including 2,000 women, working on the railways and in the yards and offices by 1943. That number comprised only eleven thousand people less than Wilmington's entire population on the eve of the war. The influx of workers was so great that three new housing projects—Maffitt Village, Lake Forest, and Hillcrest—were developed to handle the overflow.

The North Carolina Shipbuilding Company mostly constructed two basic models of vessels to carry much needed supplies, provisions, and equipment to U.S. armed forces overseas. Between 1941 and 1943, the shipyard turned out 126 "Liberty ships," as they became popularly known. They proved to be indispensable cargo vessels, although considered the "ugly ducklings" of the U.S. merchant fleet.

✧

On December 6, 1941, the Wilmington Shipbuilding Company launched its first Liberty ship, the USS Zebulon B. Vance, *named for one of North Carolina's Civil War governors.*

COURTESY OF ANNA PENNINGTON.

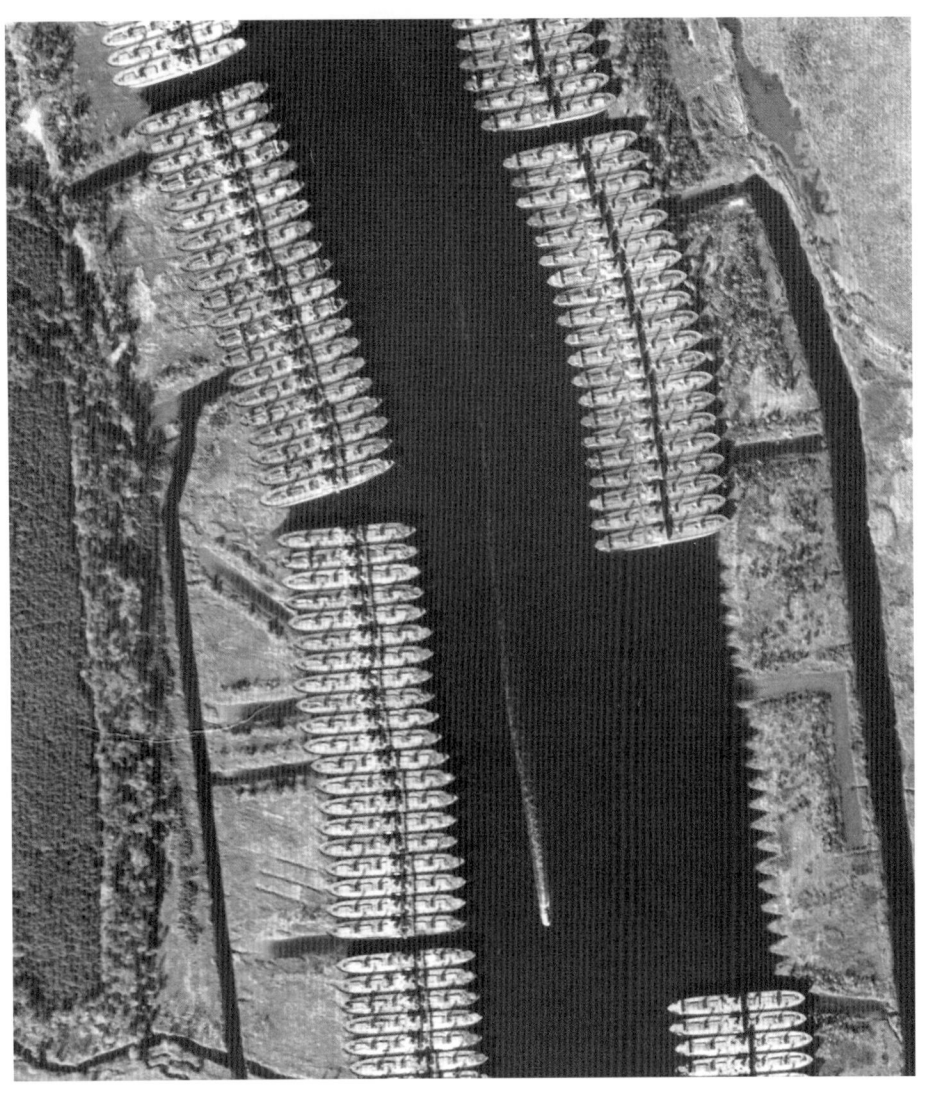

Above: A mothballed fleet of World War II Liberty ships on the Brunswick River near Wilmington.
COURTESY OF THE CAPE FEAR MUSEUM.

Right: Typical of the prefab Liberty ships built in Wilmington under the auspices of the U.S. Maritime Commission during World War II was the USS Edward B. Dudley. *She was 441 feet long, 56 feet wide, powered by a three-cylinder reciprocating steam engine capable of a speed of 11 knots, and could carry 9,000 tons of cargo, including airplanes, tanks, jeeps, and ammunition. Launched on February 13, 1943, the* Edward B. Dudley *was sunk by a German submarine in the Atlantic Ocean later that year.*
COURTESY OF STEVE MCALLISTER.

On December 6, 1941, the USS *Zebulon B. Vance*, named for one of North Carolina's Civil War governors, became the first Liberty ship launched from the Wilmington yard, which was located at the present-day site of the North Carolina Ports Authority. From 1943 to 1946, 117 faster and larger C2s were also built by the North Carolina Shipbuilding Company. In all, 243 merchant and navy cargo ships were constructed at Wilmington, greatly contributing to Allied victory by 1945.

The risks ran high in transporting supplies overseas, as convoys of merchant vessels were vulnerable to attack by enemy ships, especially submarines. In fact, one in five merchant vessels were sunk by enemy fire and the percentage of losses suffered by the merchant marines was the highest of any branch of the armed forces during World War II.

Between 1946 and 1960, 426 Liberty and other navy cargo ships were mothballed on the Brunswick River. There they remained until reactivated or broken up for scrap metal during the Vietnam War, with the last one disappearing in 1970.

The military production activity at Wilmington and the commercial shipping lanes close to the North Carolina coast soon attracted the attention of German U-boats. Not since the Civil War had enemy ships appeared off the Cape Fear. World War II made its rude appearance in the region on the night of March 12, 1942, when a torpedo from the German submarine U-158 struck the *SS John D. Gill*, an oil tanker en route from Texas to Philadelphia, sending her to the bottom of the sea off Cape Fear with the loss of 19 of her 42 crewmen. With the sinking of the SS *John D. Gill*, the Cape Fear became a war zone.

The most brazen and mysterious enemy attack at the Cape Fear occurred the following year. Urban legend purports that in the early

morning hours of July 25, 1943, a German U-boat surfaced to fire its deck gun at the Ethyl-Dow Chemical Company plant at Kure Beach on Federal Point eighteen miles south of Wilmington. The Ethyl-Dow plant, which operated from 1937 until 1946, produced ethylene out of bromide from sea water for high octane fuel. Although no hard evidence has been uncovered to substantiate the audacious attack, workers at the plant claimed to have witnessed it. A. B. Love, Jr., recalled that five shots were fired from the Nazi submarine, all of which flew harmlessly over the factory before landing in Brunswick County on the opposite side of the Cape Fear River. Ralph T. Horton, Haywood Moore, Dan Odom, Billy High and other employees supported Love's story with eyewitness accounts of their own. Thorough research by Wilbur D. Jones, Jr., the authority on Wilmington during World War II, has convinced him that the story is true and may have been the only enemy attack on the Atlantic coastline during the war.

Most Wilmingtonians were unaware of the alleged bombardment until war's end, although there had been a general blackout in the area that night. Whether the attack occurred or not, the vulnerability of key industrial targets led to increased security. Military planes flew up and down the coast during the day to spot for German submarines, while coast guard personnel made nightly patrols, often on horseback, along the beaches to prevent enemy saboteurs from coming ashore under the cover of darkness. Civilians also contributed to the reconnaissance efforts. James C. "Skinny" Pennington and his wife Anna of Pennington's Flying Service helped organize the Wilmington Civil Air Patrol to conduct anti-submarine patrols.

To further safeguard its Cape Fear industrial facilities and to prepare soldiers for combat overseas, the U.S. Army established anti-aircraft training and coastal defense bases in the area. In early December 1941, the government took over the Wilmington airport and converted it into Bluethenthal Field Army Air Base for anti-submarine aircraft and as a P-47 Thunderbolt training area. The field was named in honor of Sergeant Arthur Bluethenthal, a popular Wilmington-born aviator killed in action while serving with the Lafayette Flying Corps during the First World War. Bluethenthal Field has since been incorporated into the Wilmington International Airport.

In early 1941 the government established an enormous coast artillery and anti-aircraft training base called Camp Davis at Holly Ridge thirty miles north of Wilmington. Holly Ridge was little more than a crossroads intersection on Highway 17 in Pender County until the army moved in, occupying forty-six thousand acres of sandy ground adjacent to Holly Shelter swamp but with access to Wilmington via the Atlantic Coast Line Railroad. The desolate site allowed for unencumbered artillery and small arms firing and exercises and jungle warfare training. At the height of the war in early 1944, thirty-seven thousand soldiers, including many African Americans, were stationed at Camp Davis. Fifty-two young female pilots also served there, towing targets behind airplanes to be shot at by anti-aircraft guns on the ground. This not only

✧

Above: Wilmingtonians marvel over a Japanese mini-sub, which had been captured at Pearl Harbor, docked at Front and Market Streets during a cross-country war bonds' tour in early May 1943.
COURTESY OF THE LOWER CAPE FEAR HISTORICAL SOCIETY.

Below: Urban legend has it that the Ethyl-Dow Chemical Plant on Kure Beach was shelled by a German submarine in the early morning hours of July 25, 1943.
COURTESY OF THE NEW HANOVER PUBLIC LIBRARY.

CHAPTER VIII

55

✦

Above: African American soldiers, stationed at nearby Camp Davis in Pender County north of Wilmington, practice firing a 155-millimeter coast artillery gun out over the Atlantic Ocean in late 1941 or early 1942.
COURTESY OF THE NEW HANOVER COUNTY PUBLIC LIBRARY.

Below: More than fifty young WASPs (Women Airforce Service Pilots), whose job often required towing targets behind airplanes to be shot at by anti-aircraft guns, served at Camp Davis during World War II.
COURTESY OF DAVID STALLMAN.

freed male pilots for combat duty, but also introduced WASPs (Women Airforce Service Pilots) into the U.S. armed forces. Two WASP fliers were killed when their planes crashed at Camp Davis.

Soldiers saw "detached duty" at Fort Fisher for advanced anti-aircraft, anti-tank, and automatic weapons training. The army built barracks, storehouses, and a hospital just north of the old Confederate stronghold and cut a runway for landing small military aircraft through the fort's sand wall which can still be seen. Soldiers enjoyed their time at Fort Fisher as it afforded them the opportunity to swim in the ocean and visit nearby Carolina Beach during off-duty hours.

In addition to being a training area for U.S. soldiers, the Lower Cape Fear also served as a confinement center for German prisoners of war. Between February 1944 and April 1946, about fourteen hundred German officers and enlisted men were held in four local camps. The first one was located outside the city limits on the southeast corner of Shipyard Boulevard and Carolina Beach Road. That camp closed when a second, more conveniently located camp was opened in a four-square block area surrounding the old Marine Hospital at Eighth and Nun Streets in Wilmington. A satellite camp was established at Bluethenthal Army Air Base. The largest number of POWs, however, were confined at Camp Davis in Holly Ridge. The German soldiers, with the exception of officers, were put to work in fertilizer plants, lumber factories, and on dairy and flower farms to bolster the shortage of laborers due to the war.

Wilmingtonians were concerned about the appearance of enemy soldiers in their midst, especially those who resided near the Marine Hospital camp. Adults warned young people to stay away from the Germans confined inside the barbed wire compound. Margaret Sampson Rogers, who attended Williston Primary School across the street from the POW camp, recalled being taught to climb trees in the event of an enemy escape attempt. Parents tried to allay the fears of their children by making a game out of it called "hiding from the wolf." In the end, however, the German prisoners turned out to be docile, disciplined, and hard-working. Some of them even established good relationships with families for whom they worked and kept in touch with them after the war.

The German prisoners of war caused no interruption to the social life in Wilmington and nearby beach towns, which was so important to boosting the morale of military personnel stationed in the Cape Fear as well as the local economy. Servicemen and civilians alike flocked to downtown Wilmington to cut loose on Friday and Saturday nights. At the height of the war almost 100,000 military personnel and civilians resided in New Hanover County alone, more than doubling the prewar population of 46,000 people. White servicemen

Top: Citizens, servicemen, and automobiles packed Front Street in downtown Wilmington in 1942, as Casablanca, starring Humphrey Bogart and Ingrid Bergman, appeared at the plush Bailey Theater.
COURTESY OF THE NEW HANOVER COUNTY PUBLIC LIBRARY.

Middle: White servicemen frequented the United Service Organization's club at Second and Orange Streets in downtown Wilmington. Historic preservationists have saved the building, one of only a few remaining in the country.
COURTESY OF THE NEW HANOVER COUNTY PUBLIC LIBRARY.

Bottom, left: Soldiers and their dates "dance to the music" at the Bluethenthal Army Air Base (now part of the Wilmington International Airport) near Wilmington.
COURTESY OF WILBUR D. JONES, JR.

Bottom, right: Blonde bombshell and popular "pin-up girl" Betty Grable visited Wilmington and Camp Davis in August 1942 to remind the boys of what they were really fighting for.
COURTESY OF WILBUR D. JONES, JR.

CHAPTER VIII

Above: Gridironers at Camp Davis practice during off-duty hours for a big game.
COURTESY OF THE NEW HANOVER COUNTY PUBLIC LIBRARY.

Below: Boyhood friends from Wilmington and former Virginia Military Institute roommates Lieutenant Chris E. "Gene" Fonvielle, Seventh Armored Division (right), and Captain Dan D. Cameron, 430th AAA Battalion, reunited at Ludwigsburg, Germany in 1945.
COURTESY OF CHRIS E. FONVIELLE, JR.

packed local USO (United Service Organizations) clubs at Second and Orange Streets in Wilmington, and at Carolina Beach and in Southport.

Racial segregation compelled African Americans to attend a separate USO club at Ninth and Nixon Streets in Wilmington, as well as other entertainment places. Blacks frequented the popular Green Lantern Tavern on Campbell Street and "the Barn," a jazz hot spot at Eleventh and Meares Streets. Hundreds of people packed the Barn on weekend nights to hear some of the finest musicians of the day including Duke Ellington, Count Basie, Lionel Hampton, Billy Eckstein, and Ella Fitzgerald.

If soldiers could not get off base to attend dances, listen to their favorite bands, or see celebrities in town, then the performers came to them. Sexy pin-up actress Betty Grable performed with the USO show "Hollywood Follies" for a war bond rally in Wilmington and at Camp Davis in late August 1942, and heavyweight boxing champion Joe Louis fought an exhibition bout at Camp Davis on January 22, 1944. Despite the popularity of the blonde bombshell and the "Brown Bomber," however, the largest turn-out of soldiers was for a football game between Wake Forest College and Camp Davis on September 22, 1943. A crowd of twenty thousand people watched Wake Forest suffer its first defeat of the season, thanks in part to the play of Camp Davis's John G. Mellus, a former All-Pro tackle with the New York Giants of the NFL before the war.

When all was said and done, World War II, like all wars, was about fighting, and about fifty thousand soldiers trained at Camp Davis alone before being shipped off to combat in Europe and in the Pacific. When the war finally ended in 1945, veterans began coming home from overseas, Gene Fonvielle and Dan Cameron among them. Happy to have survived the conflict and now reunited, the two old friends bought property next to each other and built houses for their young brides in Beaumont, a residential neighborhood under development in east Wilmington. There they would remain for many years, living their lives, raising children, providing for their families, and contributing to their community like hundreds of other veterans of the Cape Fear's Greatest Generation.

Chapter IX

Wilmington Yesterday and Today

Wilmington's growth and development slowed considerably in the years immediately following World War II. The city's unprecedented rate of expansion during the conflict could not be sustained, and things reverted to a more normal pace as the military demobilized and the shipyard downsized after victory in 1945. In fact, for a brief time Wilmington almost went back to being the provincial town it had been before 1840. The slowdown actually began in the late nineteenth century when the center of economic and political power migrated into the piedmont area of North Carolina. After that time, the state's rampant growth occurred in Raleigh, Durham, Greensboro, Charlotte, and Winston-Salem. The impending shift was interrupted only by the military and industrial activities in Wilmington during both World War I and World War II.

A certain simplicity and peacefulness characterized Wilmington in the late 1940s and early 1950s. The boys of '41 returned home from the war as men throughout late 1945 and into 1946, readjusting to civilian life at their own pace. They went back to work—many of them in family-owned businesses—got married, built homes, and started having children of the baby-boomer generation. Dairies still delivered milk and butter to homes whose owners kept their backdoors unlocked so the milkman could enter in the pre-dawn hours without disturbing family members who were more than likely still asleep. Few people locked the doors to their homes at all, even if they planned to spend the day in town or at the beach. When making local phone calls, residents merely picked up the receiver and asked the female operator, who most callers knew by name, to connect them with the party to whom they wished to speak. If the person was not at home, the operator oftentimes knew where to find them around town. All of that would soon change.

In the wake of humanity's most destructive war, Wilmingtonians determined to celebrate life by accentuating the region's rich history, culture, natural beauty, and art. The Azalea Festival, named for the beautiful flower that blooms for only a few weeks in early spring, was established only three

The Cape Fear River and adjacent marshes in all their splendor as they appear from Orton Cove at the Brunswick Town-Fort Anderson State Historic Site on a cool autumn day.

COURTESY OF CHRIS E. FONVIELLE, JR.

Above: Wilmington has changed a lot since this photograph was taken at the intersection of Front and Market Streets in the days before the automobile, probably about 1900.

COURTESY OF STEVE MCALLISTER.

Below: Looking northward from Third and Market Streets in downtown Wilmington, the Colonial Hotel (burned down in 1962), the Courthouse, and City Hall as they appeared about 1905.

COURTESY OF THE LOWER CAPE FEAR HISTORICAL SOCIETY.

years after World War II ended. Held annually in early April, the festival features the coronation of a queen, parade, garden tour, concerts, Hollywood celebrities, dignitaries, pageantry, and all things Southern. The Azalea Festival soon became an annual ritual that now attracts tens of thousands of visitors to the city each year.

Wilmingtonians needed something to celebrate when, on December 15, 1955, referred to as "Black Thursday," the Atlantic Coast Line Railroad announced that it planned to transfer its headquarters from the Tar Heel port to Jacksonville, Florida. Wilmington's nineteenth century railroads had been integrated into the Atlantic Coast Line in 1900, which was, for much of the twentieth century, the city's largest employer. Despite civic leaders' best efforts, they could not dissuade the railroad's board of directors from relocating. The ACLRR's departure by July 1960 was a devastating blow to Wilmington, the commercial sector of which became a virtual ghost town. This was exacerbated by the flight of many families to the city's suburbs, followed soon thereafter by many businesses. Not since the yellow fever epidemic of 1862 were Wilmington's downtown streets and sidewalks so vacant and quiet. The saying was that you could fire a cannon on Front Street, the main business artery, and not hit anyone.

A group of concerned businessmen, led by Mayor Dan D. Cameron, immediately organized as the Committee of 100 to address the region's economic challenges by recruiting new businesses and industry. Hugely successful, the organization convinced General Electric, DuPont, W. R. Grace, Corning, and smaller companies to set up shop in the Wilmington area. The city government, meanwhile, began an urban renewal project in 1965, to upgrade facilities in an effort to attract businesses. Unfortunately, many historic buildings and homes fell victim to this perceived vision of progress.

To help train professionals as well as technicians, Wilmington established institutions of higher education. In 1947, citizens of New Hanover County approved a tax levy and Wilmington College was opened under the supervision of the New Hanover County Board of Education. Originally housed in Issac Bear School across from New Hanover High School on Market Street, the college moved out to South College Road in 1961. From only a few buildings and instructors and hundreds of students, the school became the University of North Carolina at Wilmington in 1969 that today employs more than 1,800 faculty and staff, teaches 12,500 students, and consistently ranks among the top ten universities in the South. Williston College, a branch of Williston High School, taught African American students until Wilmington College integrated in 1962. Three years earlier, the Wilmington Industrial Education Center had been established, which soon became Cape Fear Technical Institute. Since

1988, the school has been part of North Carolina's community college system as Cape Fear Community College. More recently, Brunswick Community College was founded to help meet the educational needs of Brunswick County's students.

Wilmington remained North Carolina's most active seaport after World War II. In 1946 the North Carolina State Ports Authority gained control of the North Carolina Shipbuilding facilities south of Wilmington. Even so, trade and communication with the interior of the state was hindered by the lack of sufficient roads. For years local politicians and promoters pushed for construction of a major highway linking Wilmington with Raleigh and other points inland. They finally overcame intense political and economic obstacles to extend Interstate 40 to the seaport by 1990.

Supporters saw the completion of I 40 as a boon for the future of Wilmington and southeastern North Carolina and, indeed, the rapid growth and development of the area in recent years has borne out those predictions. The secret of the Cape Fear's good life is out. Thousands of people have discovered the beauty, charm, and serenity of the region, and are moving to the area in droves, bringing cultural and ethnic diversity the likes of which have not been witnessed since antebellum days. The population of New Hanover, Brunswick, and Pender counties has soared beyond expectations, as have property values, and the local economy continues to outpace both state and national gains.

No longer are shipping and traditional industries the biggest money-makers in the region, however. Tourism has supplanted them, accounting for $375 million to the economies of New Hanover and Brunswick counties alone in 2005. By the late 1950s, promoters recognized the growing interest that heritage tourism could play in the new economy of southeastern North Carolina. With that in mind, James S. Craig, Jr., led the charge to save the World War II battleship USS North Carolina from being scrapped and bring it to Wilmington as a memorial to North

Carolinians who fought in the war. Craig enlisted the assistance of Hugh Morton, Jr., a native Wilmingtonian, owner and developer of Grandfather Mountain, and one of the state's leading tourism advocates. Generous donors and even school children, who collected pennies, nickels, and dimes, raised enough money to preserve the ship. On October 2, 1961, the North Carolina slowly made her way up the Cape Fear River, as tens of thousands of people, clapping and cheering, lined the riverbank to welcome her to her new home.

The USS North Carolina is only one of many popular tourist attractions in the Lower Cape Fear today. Carolina, Kure, Topsail, Wrightsville, and Oak Island's beaches are all packed from Memorial Day to Labor Day each year. Fort Fisher State Historic Site is one of the most visited historic place in North Carolina. Thousands of tourists also enjoy the

✧

Left: Wilmington was a railroad town from 1840 until 1960, when the Atlantic Coast Line Railroad, its complex of shops and warehouses seen in this aerial view of the general area around Front and Red Cross Streets about 1950, moved its headquarters to Jacksonville, Florida.
COURTESY OF THE NEW HANOVER COUNTY PUBLIC LIBRARY.

Below: UNC Wilmington has come a long way since this aerial view was made of its earlier incarnation, Wilmington College, in 1962. From only three buildings—Alderman Hall, Hoggard Hall, and James Hall—about seventy faculty and staff, and a few hundred students in the early 1960s, UNC Wilmington now boasts approximately 60 structures, 1,800 faculty and staff, 12,500 students, and a consistent top-ten ranking among universities in the South.
COURTESY OF UNC WILMINGTON.

✧

Above: Hurricane Hazel, the most destructive storm to hit the Cape Fear in the twentieth century, roars ashore at Kure Beach on the morning of October 15, 1954.
COURTESY OF THE LOWER CAPE FEAR HISTORICAL SOCIETY.

Right: Beautiful gardens and rich history attract thousands of visitors each year to Orton Plantation, the Cape Fear's only surviving colonial rice plantation open to the public, located in Brunswick County about fifteen miles south of Wilmington.
COURTESY OF THE SAMUEL BISSETTE COLLECTION, NEW HANOVER COUNTY PUBLIC LIBRARY.

Fort Fisher Aquarium, Brunswick Town-Fort Anderson State Historic Site, Orton Plantation, Cape Fear Museum, Wrightsville Beach Museum, Bellamy Mansion Museum, Burgwin-Wright House, and the Latimer House, the headquarters of the Lower Cape Fear Historical Society.

Even Hollywood has discovered the Lower Cape Fear. Many feature movies have been filmed in the area, including *Firestarter*, *Steel Magnolias*, *Sleeping with the Enemy*, and *Black Knight*, as well as television shows like *Matlock*, *Dawson's Creek*, and *One Tree Hill*, leading Wilmington to be dubbed "Hollywood East" and "Wilmywood."

The rampant expansion and development of Wilmington and the Lower Cape Fear is not without its critics, however, especially among people who are native to the area and remember "Old Wilmington." They point to the uncontrolled growth, congestion, pollution, and threats to both the environment and historic features. Indeed, developers recently demolished historic Babies Hospital on Wrightsville Sound and the Ice House, which dated back to the late 1830s, in downtown Wilmington.

Yet for all the challenges and setbacks Wilmington and the Lower Cape Fear have faced through the years, the area has survived and improved. Wars, riots, storms, and pestilence have been no match for the unflinching spirit of the people who have called the Lower Cape Fear home. And the lifeblood of it all has always been the Cape Fear River.

✧

Top: Old and new juxtaposed as the World War II battleship USS North Carolina *passed the remains of the colonial town of Brunswick as she ascended the Cape Fear River on October 2, 1961, toward her permanent berth at Wilmington.*
COURTESY OF THE LOWER CAPE FEAR HISTORICAL SOCIETY.

Middle: Wilmington's stately skyline as seen through the lens of the late Samuel Bissette, looking southward from atop the Murchison Building on the corner of Front and Chestnut Streets in 1997.
COURTESY OF THE SAMUEL BISSETTE COLLECTION, NEW HANOVER COUNTY PUBLIC LIBRARY.

Bottom: The United Daughters of the Confederacy erected this imposing monument at Fort Fisher in 1932, to commemorate the soldiers who defended the key fortification that protected Wilmington, the South's main seaport during the Civil War. Fort Fisher officially became a state historic site in 1962.
COURTESY OF THE SAMUEL BISSETTE COLLECTION, NEW HANOVER COUNTY PUBLIC LIBRARY.

CHAPTER XI

Appendix

Sports, Recreation and Entertainment in the Lower Cape Fear

Above: Horse racing reached the height of its popularity in the South during antebellum days. The Wilmington Daily Journal *advertised a series of upcoming late autumn races at the Clarendon Course, which was located east of Wilmington off the New Bern Road. In the four day affair, December 18-21, 1844, R. Fenner's blood horse Oregon and J. Bulloch's black filly Miss Chester won most of the heats and prize money. Oregon emerged as the fastest horse overall, beating Miss Chester in three out of five heats on the final day of the races.*

Above: Thalian Hall quickly became a favorite destination for Wilmington theater-goers when it opened its doors to the public in mid-October 1858, almost three years after construction began. Built onto the rear of City Hall at Third and Princess Streets, Thalian Hall accommodated 1,000 people, about 10 percent of the town's population at the time. It was designed by John M. Trimble of New York, a leading theater architect in nineteenth century America. James F. Post of Wilmington served as supervising architect, while Robert B. and John C. Wood, and George W. Rose constructed the building. Many famous actors and actresses have performed at Thalian Hall in the past 149 years. Foremost among the nineteenth century actors was Joseph Jefferson III, pictured above, whose role as Rip Van Winkle, the character in Washington Irving's tale who slept for twenty years, made him famous.

COURTESY OF THE LOWER CAPE FEAR HISTORICAL SOCIETY.

Left: Three African American boys crouch in awe and amazement beside a large alligator killed along Wilmington's waterfront about 1875. From colonial days, shooting the prehistoric-looking reptiles was considered sport. Hunted almost to extinction, alligators have made a comeback in the Cape Fear since state and federal laws were passed, beginning in the late 1960s, to protect them.

COURTESY OF THE NEW HANOVER PUBLIC LIBRARY.

Below: Wilmingtonians enjoyed taking pleasure trips on board steamboats down the Cape Fear River from the time the earliest steam vessels, Henrietta *and* Prometheus, *first appeared in the region in 1818. This candid snapshot by an unidentified photographer shows the excursion boat* Seagate, *which plied the Cape Fear from 1904 to 1907, pulling up to the Wilmington waterfront between Market and Dock Streets. The Wilmington, Southport & Little River Transportation Company owned the* Seagate *until it was sold off to a plantation owner in Savannah, Georgia.*

COURTESY OF CHRIS E. FONVIELLE, JR.

Above: Enthusiastic young men began organizing football teams in Wilmington by the early 1890s, with Hilton Park on the city's north side being a regular field of play. The earliest extant photograph of a Wilmington "eleven," as teams were often called in those days, shows "shaggy-haired players [of Wilmington High School] in full battle array" (note the nose guards strapped around some of the boys' necks). Identifiable are Professor John J. Blair (tall man standing in the rear), Manager N. S. McLaurin (shorter man standing in the back), Captain Leslie Wiggs (seated in the front holding the pigskin, which is dated 1898-1899), and McLaurin's Gordon setter "Fitzhugh Lee," the team mascot. Also pictured, but not identified, were team members Frank Culbreth, Malcome Parker, Willie Grant, Joe Laughlin, Edwin Bunting, Harry Smallbones, Jr., Thomas J. Gause, Russell Foster, Willie Moore, and Arthur Schilken. The photograph was taken, according to the Wilmington Messenger, *on February 10, 1899.*

COURTESY OF THE LOWER CAPE FEAR HISTORICAL SOCIETY.

Above: A broadside advertisement for excursion voyages on board the steamboat City of Southport, *which made daily runs between Wilmington, Southport, and Fort Caswell on Oak Island at the mouth of the Cape Fear River in the late 1920s and early 1930s. Built as the* Isleboro *in Rockland, Maine in 1914, she saw service as an excursion vessel on the Hudson River in New York before being purchased by Captain Leta Dosher Potter of Wilmington, North Carolina in 1926. Upon the* Isleboro's *arrival at the Tar Heel seaport in May 1927, she was renamed the* City of Southport *and readied for passenger and freight service on the Cape Fear River. The steamboat measured 75 feet in length, drew 7 feet of water, and safely carried about 150 passengers. She made regular runs up and down the river until at least 1932, after which time the Great Depression compelled Captain Potter to retire the boat. Potter died in 1934, having never lost a passenger in more than fifty years as a riverboat captain.*

COURTESY OF STEVE MCALLISTER.

Above: A sailing expedition in the Lower Cape Fear about 1875.

COURTESY OF THE BELLAMY MANSION MUSEUM.

Above: The grandest twentieth century attraction at Wrightsville Beach, located nine miles east of Wilmington, was Lumina. Consolidated Railways, Light & Power Company (later known as the Tide Water Power Company) built the pavilion along the oceanfront at Station # 7 on its electric rail line in 1905. When Lumina opened its doors to the public on June 3 of that year, it quickly became the favorite destination for beachgoers and tourists. It featured a large ballroom for big bands and dancing, bowling alley, game arcade, moving pictures, athletic and aquatic competitions and beauty contests. Due to the enormous success of Lumina, Tide Water Power expanded the facilities and attractions in 1909, making Lumina more popular than ever. In its early days, the pavilion was illuminated from the roof to the ground by hundreds of tungsten lights which could be seen for miles, leading it to be known as the "Palace of Light." Sadly, Lumina was demolished in April 1973 to make way for residential townhouses. Shown here was the expanded Lumina looking north from the sound-side about 1910.

COURTESY OF THE NEW HANOVER COUNTY PUBLIC LIBRARY.

Above: The Lower Cape Fear has produced many great and famous athletes, including Meadowlark Lemon, Sam Bowen, Althea Gibson, Sunny Jurgensen, Roman Gabriel, Michael Jordan, Clyde Simmons, and Trot Nixon. One of the less well known athletes, but by all accounts one of the very best, was Charlie Niven of Wilmington. Leon Brogden, legendary coach at New Hanover High School from 1945 to 1969, described Charlie Niven as the most gifted athlete he ever coached, including Jurgensen and Gabriel. Niven played on the NHHS Wildcats football, basketball, and baseball teams from 1946 to 1950, earning the nickname, "speed demon." In his senior year, Niven was named all-conference and all-state running back in football and was invited to play in the annual Shrine Bowl game. After high school, Niven played one year of football at Duke University and one year for the Edmonton Eskimos in the Canadian Football League, before returning to his hometown.

COURTESY OF SHERRY NIVEN.

Above: Although immensely popular worldwide for centuries, organized soccer did not appear in the Lower Cape Fear until the 1960s. Alex Weide, a lieutenant in the German navy during World War II who immigrated to Wilmington in 1949, put together a team at New Hanover High School in 1967. Weide's early squads played against all comers, including teams from UNC Wilmington, Southeastern Community College in Whiteville, North Carolina, and foreign ships that visited the port city. The New Hanover High School Wildcat soccer team seen here won the inter-high school conference title in only its second year of play in 1968, but lost in the state playoffs to Camp Lejune High School, a team it had beaten four times during the regular season. Front row (from left to right): Larry Soles, Coach Alex Weide, Chris E. Fonvielle, Jr., Jackie Blackmore, Sam Eckhardt, Bob Spencer. Second row: Charlie Halterman, Stewart Keels, Wayne Bland, Barney Lewis, Bill Renn, Richard Wilson, Walter Futch. Third row: Fred Ourt, Sammy Norris, Woody Henderson, David "Lightning" Smith, Norman Brooks, Gill Buffington, Tom Milsakowski, Charles Ostrand.

COURTESY OF NEW HANOVER HIGH SCHOOL.

Above: Anna Raynor, a senior on UNC Wilmington's track and field team, practices throwing the javelin at the school's track field. From baseballs and softballs at South Johnston High School in Benson, North Carolina to the javelin at "UNC by the Sea," Raynor has always thrown objects great distances. "I never really threw like a girl," she claims. In only her second year tossing the javelin, Raynor placed fourth in the 2006 NCAA Outdoor Track and Field Championships in Sacramento, California. She was named Colonial Athletic Association Female Athlete-of-the-Year in track and field two years in a row, 2005 and 2006, as well as All-American for the second consecutive year, making her the only female athlete at UNC Wilmington to earn that coveted award in back-to-back seasons.

COURTESY OF UNC WILMINGTON.

Above: Long before the Azalea Festival, Wilmington's hugely popular annual springtime party organized in 1948, there was the Feast of Pirates. Celebrated in August, the Feast of Pirates was initially held for only three years, 1927-1929. It was kicked-off with the coronation of a queen on the steps of City Hall on Third Street, followed by a street party and parade, motorboat races, cute baby contest, and coronation dance at Lumina on Wrightsville Beach. Perhaps the festival's most exciting event each year was the capture of the city by a shipload of swashbuckling pirate re-enactors, some of whom are pictured here on Cape Fear River as they prepare to storm ashore. A lack of funds and the ensuing Great Depression doomed the Feast of Pirates, although there were attempts to revive it in the early 1970s and again in the early 1990s.

COURTESY OF THE NEW HANOVER COUNTY PUBLIC LIBRARY.

Above: One of the pioneer surfers on the Cape Fear coast, Joe Funderburg of Wrightsville Beach, pulls into a nice wave on his way to winning the South Atlantic Surfing Championship at Carolina Beach in the autumn of 1966. Although occasional surfers were seen riding the breakers along area beaches as early as the 1920s, they were an anomaly for the next forty years. Inspired by the West Coast surfing movement in the late 1950s and early 1960s, Joe Funderburg, Robert Parker, Lank Lancaster, and other young men popularized the sport along the Cape Fear coast by 1963.

COURTESY OF THE CAPE FEAR SURFING ARCHIVE, WILLIAM RANDALL LIBRARY, UNC WILMINGTON.

Left: True to his namesake, Brett Blizzard blew up a storm of excitement in the men's basketball program at UNC Wilmington from 2000-2003. The Tallahassee, Florida native earned a host of honors for himself and his team during his four-year tenure. Considered the greatest shooter ever to play Division 1 basketball at UNCW, Blizzard became the Seahawks all-time leading scorer with 2,144 points and the first player in Colonial Athletic Association history to be named All-Conference four consecutive years. Blizzard was also named the CAA's Most Valuable Player in 2002 and 2003, and led UNC Wilmington to NCAA Tournament appearances in 2000, 2002, and 2003. Perhaps the most memorable game during Blizzard's college career was a 93-89 win over the University of Southern California, which was ranked fourth in the nation at the time, in the first round of the NCAA tournament on March 17, 2002. Blizzard scored 18 points in the contest. Since graduation, Blizzard has played professional basketball in Italy, but returned to UNC Wilmington on February 2, 2005, for a ceremony to honor his athletic achievements and retire his jersey.

COURTESY OF UNC WILMINGTON.

BIBLIOGRAPHY

Books

Barrett, John G. *The Civil War in North Carolina*. Chapel Hill: University of North Carolina Press, 1963.
Butler, Lindley S. *Pirates, Privateers, and Rebel Raiders of the Carolina Coast*. Chapel Hill: University of North Carolina Press, 2000.
Carr, Dawson. *Gray Phantoms of the Cape Fear*. Winston-Salem, North Carolina: John F. Blair, 1998.
Carson, Susan S. *Joshua's Dream: A Town With Two Names*. Southport, North Carolina: Southport Historical Society, 1994.
Cecelski, David. *The Waterman's Song: Slavery and Freedom in Maritime North Carolina*. Chapel Hill: University of North Carolina Press, 2001.
Cecelski, David and Timothy B. Tyson, eds. *Democracy Betrayed: The Wilmington Race Riot and Its Legacy*. Chapel Hill: University of North Carolina Press, 1998.
Conner, R. D. W. *Cornelius Harnett: An Essay in North Carolina History*. Raleigh, North Carolina: Edwards & Broughton Printing Co., 1909.
Curtis, W. G. *Reminiscences of Wilmington and Southport, 1848-1900*. Southport, North Carolina: Herald Job's Office, 1900.
Crow, Jeffery J., Paul D. Escott, and Flora J. Hatley, eds. *A History of African Americans in North Carolina*. Raleigh: Office of Archives and History, 1992.
DeRosset, William Lord. *Pictorial and Historical New Hanover County and Wilmington, North Carolina*. Wilmington: DeRosset, 1938.
Fonvielle, Chris E., Jr. *Fort Anderson: Battle for Wilmington*. Mason City, Iowa: Savas Publishing Company, 1999.
_____. *The Wilmington Campaign: Last Rays of Departing Hope*. Campbell, California: Savas Publishing Company, 1997.
Gould, William B., IV. *Diary of a Contraband: The Civil War Passage of a Black Sailor*. Stanford, California: Stanford University Press, 2002.
Gragg, Rod. *Confederate Goliath: The Battle of Fort Fisher*. New York: HarperCollins Publishers, 1991.
Jones, Wilbur D., Jr. *A Sentimental Journey: Memoirs of a Wartime Boomtown*. Shippensburg, Pennsylvania: White Mane Books, 2002.
_____. *The Journey Continues: The World War II Home Front*. Shippensburg, Pennsylvania: White Mane Books, 2005.
Lamb, William. *Colonel Lamb's Story of Fort Fisher*. Carolina Beach, North Carolina: Blockade Runner Museum, 1966.
Lee, Lawrence. *The Lower Cape Fear in Colonial Days*. Chapel Hill: University of North Carolina Press, 1971.
Lennon, Donald R. and Ida Brooks Kellam, eds. *The Wilmington Town Book, 1743-1778*. Raleigh: North Carolina Division of Archives and History, 1979.
Meyer, Duane. *The Highland Scots of North Carolina, 1732-1776*. Chapel Hill: University of North Carolina Press, 1957.
Moore, Louis T. *Stories Old and New of the Cape Fear Region*. Wilmington, North Carolina: Wilmington Printing Co., 1956.
Pleasants, James A., Jr. *A Bibliography of the Lower Cape Fear, North Carolina, 1860-1865*. Wilmington, North Carolina: Precision Press, 1998.
Powell, William S. *Dictionary of North Carolina Biography*. 6 vols. Chapel Hill: University of North Carolina Press, 1979-1996.
_____. *North Carolina Through Four Centuries*. Chapel Hill: University of North Carolina Press, 1989.
Prather, H. Leon, Sr. *We Have Taken a City: Wilmington Racial Massacre and Coup of 1898*. Wilmington, North Carolina: Associated University Press, 1998.
Reaves, William S. *Strength Through Struggle: The Chronological and Historical Record of the African American Community in Wilmington, North Carolina, 1865-1950*. Wilmington, North Carolina: New Hanover County Public Library, 1998.
Rights, Douglas L. *The American Indian in North Carolina*. Winston-Salem, North Carolina: John F. Blair, 1957.
Seapker, Janet K., ed. *Time, Talent, Tradition. Five Essays on the Cultural History of the Lower Cape Fear Region, North Carolina*. Wilmington, 1995.
Schaw, Janet. *Journal of a Lady of Quality*. New Haven, Connecticut: Yale University Press, 1939.
Sprunt, James. *Chronicles of the Cape Fear River 1660-1916*. Raleigh, North Carolina: Edwards & Broughton Printing Co., 1916.
_____. *Tales and Traditions of the Lower Cape Fear, 1661-1896*. Wilmington, North Carolina: LeGwin Brothers, 1896.
Tetterton, Beverly. *Wilmington: Lost But Not Forgotten*. Wilmington, North Carolina: Dram Tree Books, 2005.
Thomas, Cornelius M. D. *James Forte*. Wilmington, North Carolina: Clarendon Imprint No. 3, 1959.
Waddell, Alfred Moore. *A History of New Hanover County and the Lower Cape Fear Region, 1723-1800*. Wilmington, North Carolina, n.p. 1909.
Walker, James L., Jr. *Rebel Gibraltar: Fort Fisher and Wilmington, C. S. A.* Wilmington, North Carolina: Dram Tree Books, 2005.
Watson, Alan D. *African Americans in Early North Carolina: A Documentary History*. Raleigh: Office of Archives and History, 2005.
_____. *Internal Improvements in Antebellum North Carolina*. Raleigh:: Office of Archives and History, 2002.
_____. *Wilmington: Port of North Carolina*. Columbia: University of South Carolina Press, 1992.
_____. *Wilmington, North Carolina to 1861*. Jefferson, North Carolina: McFarland & Company, Inc., 2003.
Watson, Alan D., Dennis R. Lawson, and Donald R. Lennon. *Harnett, Hooper and Howe: Revolutionary Leaders of the Lower Cape Fear*. Wilmington, North Carolina: Lower Cape Fear Historical Society, 1979.
Wise, Stephen R. *Lifeline of the Confederacy: Blockade Running During the Civil War*. Columbia: University of South Carolina Press, 1988.
Wood, Bradford J. *This Remote Part of the World: Regional Formation in the Lower Cape Fear, North Carolina, 1725-1775*. Columbia: University of South Carolina Press, 2004.
Wrenn, Tony. *Wilmington, North Carolina: An Architectural and Historical Portrait*. Charlottesville: University Press of Virginia, 1984.

Articles

Green, William J. "Spanish Raids on the Coast of North Carolina, 1741-1748." *Tributaries*, 2 (1992).
Lee, E. Lawrence. "Old Brunswick, the Story of a Colonial Town." *North Carolina Historical Review*, 29 (April 1952).
Massay, Gregory De Van. "The British Expedition to Wilmington, January—November, 1781. *North Carolina Historical Review*, 66 (1989).
McEachern, Leora H. and Isabel M. Williams. "Miss Buie, The Soldiers' Friend." *Lower Cape Fear Historical Society Bulletin* (October 1974).
Rankin, Hugh F. "The Moore's Creek Bridge Campaign, 1776." *North Carolina Historical Review*, 30 (1953).

Newspapers

Wilmington Daily Journal
Wilmington Daily Review
Wilmington Star News

❖

Since colonial days, the lifeblood of Wilmington and the Lower Cape Fear has been the river itself, as seen in this 1997 photograph of the waterway and the Cape Fear Memorial Bridge.

COURTESY OF THE SAMUEL BISSETTE COLLECTION, THE NEW HANOVER COUNTY PUBLIC LIBRARY.

SHARING THE HERITAGE

historic profiles of businesses, organizations, and families that have contributed to the development and economic base of Lower Cape Fear

Cooperative Bank	70
Wilmington Health Associates	74
Cape Fear Community College	78
Bald Head Island	81
Security Savings Bank	82
Lower Cape Fear Historical Society	85
Wilmington Surgical Associates	86
Z. A. Sneeden	88
Brunswick Community College	90
New Hanover Health Network	92
Plantation Village	94
Wilmington Development Co., Inc.	95

SPECIAL THANKS TO

McAnderson's, Inc.

Cooperative Bank

The legacy of Cooperative Bank began in 1898 when a group of prominent businessmen established and incorporated Cooperative Building and Loan Association in Wilmington. The incorporators were George L. Pescheau; Thomas H. Wright; DuBrutz Cutler, Jr.; D. O'Conner; John M. Wright; E. Payson Willard; and Walker Taylor.

The company's original mission was "to create a safe haven for depositors and provide customers a way that they might purchase homes."

Thomas H. Wright served as secretary and manager until 1933 when he was succeeded by Frederick Willetts, Sr. A native of England, Willetts had immigrated to Canada and, eventually, to Wilmington where he began a distinguished business career.

At the time Willetts was appointed manager, the nation was mired in the worst economic depression in history and Cooperative Building and Loan had assets of $330,000.

During the Depression, most families in the Wilmington area lacked cash to purchase a home and practically no credit facilities were available to them. Long-term loans with moderate installments were badly needed and Cooperative began to aggressively market this service.

The firm continued to grow despite the lean economic times and, in 1936, Willetts was elected president of the North Carolina Savings & Loan League. A year later, Cooperative received national recognition for operating thirty-nine consecutive years without a loss. In 1939, Cooperative was approved by the State of North Carolina to accept trust funds. The following year, the firm was granted permission to provide insurance coverage for savings accounts.

Assets of Cooperative reached the $1-million mark during 1941 and in 1944 the firm began offering war bonds and government bonds to help support the war effort.

Willetts was elected president and secretary-treasurer of Cooperative in 1946, becoming the first of three generations of Willetts to lead the organization. He was also elected a member of the Federal Home Loan Bank Board.

Cooperative purchased the Firestone Building on Wilmington's Front Street in 1946 and moved into its new home office in 1948, the year of Wilmington's first Azalea Festival.

The firm's name was changed from Cooperative Building and Loan Association to Cooperative Savings and Loan Association on December 1, 1948. About this time a national survey revealed that Cooperative was one of the soundest savings and loans in North Carolina.

The postwar years saw a boom in housing demand as soldiers returned from the war eager to start families and settle into a more peaceful lifestyle. This fueled the demand for

❖
Above: Frederick Willetts, Sr.

Below: The lobby of the Cooperative Bank location at 124 Princess Street in 1932.

home loans and, in 1950, Cooperative reached the $2-million milestone in funds lent for purchasing, building, or remodeling homes.

During this period, Cooperative shareholders were enjoying one of the highest savings rates in the country—three percent—insured by the Federal Savings and Loan Insurance Corporation.

The postwar business boom encouraged Cooperative's management to develop more aggressive plans for expanding its products and markets.

The bank established a branch office in Jacksonville in February 1954, the first savings & loan branch in North Carolina. A third office was established in Wallace in May. This was the same year Hurricane Hazel devastated Wrightsville Beach, Carolina Beach, Oak Island, and large sections of North Carolina.

In 1955, Willetts was elected president of the Southeastern Conference of the U.S. Savings & Loan League. The association continued to grow during this period and by December 1957 the firm had reached $15 million in assets. The savings rate increased also—to three-and-one-half percent.

A fourth Cooperative office was opened in Morehead City in June 1958. The following May, the Association was authorized to make FHA loans.

A community-wide celebration on August 31, 1959, marked the opening of Cooperative's new home office building at Second and Market Streets in Wilmington. This building included large conference rooms available for public use and a carillon on which noted carillonneurs performed. The spacious lobby featured a wishing well that collected contributions for local charities.

Cooperative also commissioned Roy Gussow to create a memorable sculpture, *Desire in Motion*, to be placed at the corner of Second and Market Streets. The 6-$\frac{1}{2}$-foot-tall sculpture rested on a 12-foot base of black granite. During dedication ceremonies, Cooperative President Willetts said the sculpture reflected Cooperative's desire "to improve the standard of living by providing better homes."

In 1961, Cooperative opened offices in Elizabethtown and Tabor City. The lending limits of Cooperative were extended to all of Bladen, Columbus, and Duplin Counties in 1962.

Willetts, who was the association's leader for thirty years, died in 1963. His son, Frederick Willetts, Jr., succeeded him as president, chief executive officer, and manager.

As a tribute to Willetts, a beautiful water garden was constructed and dedicated to the citizens of Wilmington. It continues to attract visitors to downtown Wilmington even today.

Cooperative continued to grow in the 1960s under the leadership of Fred, Jr. A state-of-the-art computer system was installed and, to stay competitive in the marketplace, interest rates on savings accounts were raised, compounded, and paid quarterly.

In 1967, the year New Hanover Memorial Hospital opened, Cooperative's assets exceeded $51 million. CS&L Services Corporation was established in the early 1970s as a wholly owned subsidiary of Cooperative. This allowed the bank to purchase land, sell lots and act as a holding company and was used to develop land throughout the area.

Fred, Jr. was elected president of the North Carolina Savings & Loan League in 1970, the same year the Hanover Center office was opened in Wilmington.

Cooperative celebrated its seventy fifth anniversary in 1973, the same year Fred, Jr.

✧

Above: Frederick Willetts, Jr.

Below: The 1959 opening of the Market Street renovations.

✧
Frederick Willetts III.

was elected director of the Federal Home Loan Bank of Atlanta. The year also saw passbook savings rates increased to five and one-quarter percent.

Cooperative opened the Long Leaf office on College Road in Wilmington during 1974. During this period the bank went online with all its computers in the Wilmington office and assets increased to well over $100 million.

In 1975 an office was opened in Beaufort and the Association converted from a "Share" to a "Deposit" operation and began marketing Certificates of Deposit. Fred, Jr. was elected president of the Southeastern Conference of the U.S. Savings and Loan League in 1977 and, by the end of 1978, the Association had begun offering variable rate mortgages.

The late '70s also saw completion of an addition to the home office in Wilmington and the purchase of a building adjacent to the home office that was used for accounting and computer operations. The Tabor City office opened in 1980 and in 1981, Frederick, Jr. was elected to the executive committee of the U.S. Savings & Loan League. A year later, Cooperative opened the Western Boulevard office in Jacksonville.

Cooperative continued to expand in 1983 with the purchase of Seaboard Savings and Loan, a state-chartered stock savings association with assets of $60 million. The acquisition added offices in Washington, Belhaven, Robersonville, and Kill Devil Hills. An additional Washington office was opened in 1987.

Frederick "Rick" Willetts III, who had joined the firm in 1972, was elected president of the Southeastern Conference of the U.S. Savings & Loan League in 1985, the only time three generations have been elected to the same national office in the savings and loan industry.

Cooperative received national recognition for its profitability in 1986 when it was ranked tenth among the nation's savings and loans with respect to return on average assets. At the same time, Cooperative also ranked first in profitability throughout North Carolina. The year 1988 was a banner year in mortgage lending with the closing of $63 million in real estate loans.

The decade of the '90s brought accelerated change and growth for Cooperative. Frederick Willetts, Jr., retired as president in 1991, continuing as chairman of the board. Rick Willetts succeeded him as president and chief executive officer.

In a major development, Cooperative soon converted to a stock corporation, an action followed a year later by conversion to a state-chartered savings bank.

A 25 percent stock dividend was paid in 1992, followed by a 50 percent stock dividend less than a year later. In February 1994 another 50 percent stock dividend was declared and, in September 1997, a 100 percent stock dividend was paid.

This marked the fourth time the company's stock had split since the public offering in 1991. An initial investment of $1,000 at that time grew to a value of $13,720 on December 31, 1997, an annual increase of approximately 50 percent.

The year 1993 saw the opening of a loan origination office in Corolla and the establishment of a retail banking operation. This was the forerunner to the introduction of a full range of retail services, including deposit, investment and consumer as well as commercial lending. This broad scope of services qualified Cooperative as a full-service community bank.

Cooperative Bankshares, Inc., was chartered in 1994 with Cooperative Bank becoming a subsidiary. This move better positioned the organization for greater growth and influence in the region.

A new office was opened in 1995 in the Ogden area of Wilmington and, in 1997, Rick was appointed to the Thrift Institutions Advisory Council to the Federal Reserve Board. He also was elected chairman of the North Carolina Bankers Association and to the executive committee of America's Community Bankers.

During the entire year of 1998, the company celebrated its one-hundredth birthday with celebrations throughout all of its communities. Drawings for grand prizes were given at each of the financial centers and new customers received a free gift for opening a checking account.

In May 1998, Frederick Willetts, Jr. passed away. The City of Wilmington mourned this beloved citizen.

The Whiteville financial center opened for business in April 2001 and continues to be one of the bank's most successful centers. During 2002, Cooperative purchased Lumina Mortgage, Inc., which became a subsidiary of the bank. Lumina Mortgage is a banking firm, originating and selling residential mortgages in Wilmington, North Carolina; Myrtle Beach, South Carolina; and Virginia Beach, Virginia. During the same year, the company formed a real estate investment trust (REIT), which also became a subsidiary of the bank.

On December 31, 2002, Cooperative completed its conversion to a state-chartered commercial bank, thus better defining the way it does business.

Wilmington operations expanded in 2003 with the opening of new centers at Monkey Junction and Landfall Center. Morehead City opened its second location on Highway 24, and the first center in Southport opened in December, expanding for the first time into Brunswick County, the fastest growing county in North Carolina.

With the purchase of Lumina Mortgage, Cooperative employees have grown to 187 working at 24 financial centers. Assets were $496,387,147 as of September 30, 2003.

After more than a century of service, Cooperative Bank continues to grow and expand, helping thousands of customers in eastern North Carolina fulfill their dream of home ownership and reach their financial goals.

For more information on Cooperative Bank, please visit www.coop-bank.com.

✧

Above: The Memorial Water Garden at 201 Market Street in Wilmington.

Below: The Cooperative Bank one-hundred-year anniversary celebration in 1998.

SHARING THE HERITAGE

WILMINGTON HEALTH ASSOCIATES

Wilmington Health Associates began over three decades ago with two physicians and a determination to provide the finest possible medical care. That vision created a practice that has grown to more than eighty caring providers, practicing sixteen specialties in a state-of-the-art environment.

The concept for Wilmington Health Associates, one of the largest multi-specialty practices in southeastern North Carolina, actually had its beginnings over a keg of beer.

The year was 1971 and two young physicians, Dr. Dan Gottovi and Dr. Norm Robinson, were attending a conference organized by the dean of the School of Medicine at the University of North Carolina at Chapel Hill.

The purpose of the conference was to address the need for more teaching programs throughout the state. Dr. Gottovi and Dr. Robinson were each being interviewed to spearhead such a program in the Wilmington area and happened to meet in line for the beer keg.

The two began talking and Dr. Robinson quipped that working on the coast was certainly not a bad idea and that he and Dr. Gottovi should consider opening a private practice there. After all, the sailing was good and if the funding came through for an educational center, they'd be in a perfect position.

That conversation haunted Dr. Gottovi throughout the weekend and on Monday he phoned Dr. Robinson and said, "Let's do it."

The name Wilmington Health Associates was born as the two doctors drove to Wilmington on one of their initial trips to the coast.

Dr. Gottovi, a pulmonary specialist and internist, and Dr. Robinson, a cardiologist, felt the future success of the new practice lay in the ability to offer a full range of medical testing, diagnosis and treatment under one roof.

The two doctors took an ad in the Wilmington paper for staff and were overwhelmed by the number of highly qualified applicants. "We were flying by the seat of our pants at the beginning," recalls Dr. Gottovi, "but Dr. Robinson had a philosophy that kept us going. He kept saying 'If we just take really good care of the patients, everything will take care of itself.'"

That philosophy, along with a quotation from one of Dr. Gottovi's medical school professors, became a guiding principle for the new practice. Dr. Gottovi explains that the professor asked him one day how things were going. Dr. Gottovi replied, "Well, I have had some very interesting patients." The professor smiled and replied, "Remember, Mr. Gottovi, all patients are interesting patients."

Although Dr. Robinson has since retired from Wilmington Health Associates to pursue his passion for teaching, Dr. Gottovi has continued his medical practice for over thirty years.

❖

Above: Dr. Dan Gottovi in front of Wilmington Health Associates' main building located at 1202 Medical Center Drive.

Below: This artist's rendering is of the original Wilmington Health Associates office that was opened by Dr. Dan Gottovi and Dr. Norm Robinson in 1971.

Wilmington Health Associates encompasses a multitude of specialties with locations in Wilmington and surrounding areas. This is due in large part to the group's strong commitment to recruit highly trained, talented physicians and through merging with some of the top medical practices in the area including Hanover Surgical Associates, Carolina OB/Gyn and The Children's Clinic.

These groups successfully integrated their services with those of Wilmington Health's to provide comprehensive medical care to patients in not only the immediate suburban population, but also surrounding rural counties. Wilmington Health continues to offer its patients a wide range of diagnostic and screening tests including cardiac stress tests, audiology tests and services, x-ray, lab services, and screening mammography, among many others. The group also has a licensed ambulatory surgery center where colonoscopy and endoscopy procedures are performed.

Wilmington Health Associates has grown to be a major medical practice, but the core commitment to patient care and comfort are never compromised to size. The group continues to add services and expand its service area based on patient need. This concept allows patients more convenient access to medical care from where they live and work. This focus on the patient keeps Wilmington Health Associates on the leading edge of innovation and management techniques with a clear mission to continually improve patient satisfaction.

One of the many innovative programs aimed at improving patient care is deceptively simple. As part of an internationally renowned program for healthcare improvement, the practice strives to provide patients with a same-day appointment for illness and an appointment within seven days for a physical.

The real appointment, not a work-in, is usually with the patient's regular physician. The practice has a goal of maximizing face-to-face time with the patient's physician and spending no more than fifteen minutes total on activities such as check-in, wait time, and checkout.

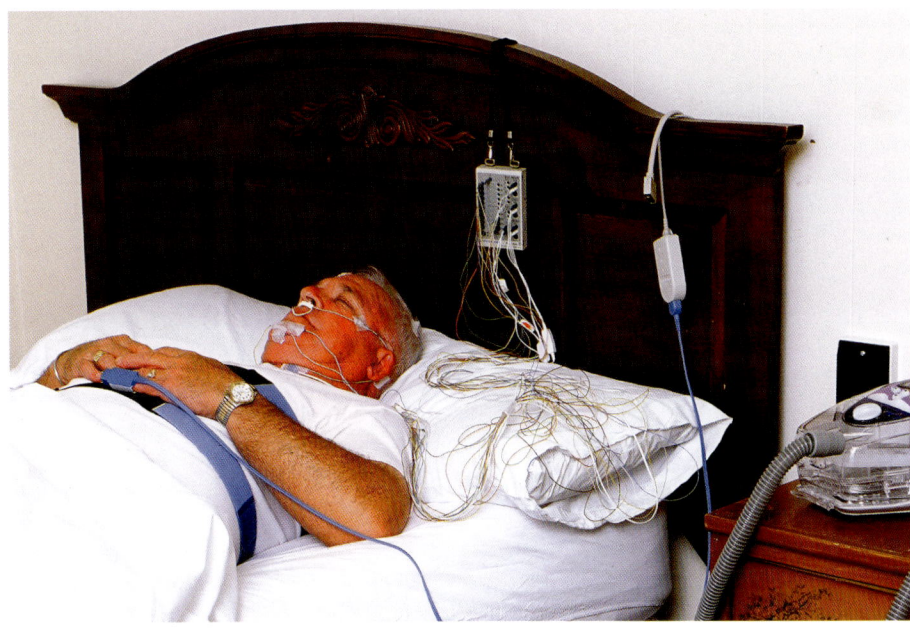

Wilmington Health introduced the program in early 2000 and since that time each participating physician has reduced their wait time for an appointment from up to 200 days to less than seven days, but generally the same day.

Another exciting initiative that began in early 2003 is implementation of an electronic medical record (also known as EMR). Wilmington Health was one of a handful of medical practices in the area to begin using such a system. The group began by implementing the EMR in stages to allow ample training time for staff and physicians. When implemented practice-wide, physicians

✧

Above: A patient is set up for a stay at the Sleep Disorder Center. The center is designed to conduct overnight and daytime sleep studies to help diagnose a wide range of sleep disorders from insomnia and sleep apnea to snoring, narcolepsy, night terrors and sleepwalking.

Below: A sleep technician closely monitors a patient's sleeping and breathing patterns, as well as their vital signs during a sleep study. Once completed a physician certified in reading sleep studies will interpret the results and provide a diagnosis for the patient.

SHARING THE HERITAGE

will use a hand-held device, similar to a laptop computer, and have a patient's medical record at their fingertips.

Much of the success of Wilmington Health Associates may be attributed to its organizational structure. The group has maintained a non-physician management team and an all-physician governing board. The governing board consists of a staggered term group of owner physicians who are elected by the member-owner physicians and are representative of various clinical divisions and specialties.

The governing board meets on a regular basis, as does the entire physician membership. Decision-making is done by physician vote, with employee physicians having input into decisions affecting their clinical departments. Committees of physicians spearhead most major projects and senior management members, working collectively as partners, all focus on the same end result–providing quality medical care.

Two members of the senior management team who work closely with the physician leadership are the executive director and the chief financial officer. While their individual roles vary, their common goal is to assist the physician leadership in making informed decisions about operational and financial issues, as well as strategic focus and planning. The executive director and chief financial

officer also work closely with the non-physician management team, which consists of directors and department managers, both clinical and non-clinical. Communication is key and maintaining it throughout the organization has always been imperative to the group's continued success.

Because of its mission to continually improve the quality of medical care and services to patients, Wilmington Health created the Patient Advisory Council. This group of about fifteen patients meets monthly for a one-hour discussion with the medical director and a member of the management team. Over the years, this process has allowed

Above: The chief financial officer and executive director review building plans and ideas for a potential new Wilmington Health location.

Below: A nuclear medicine technologist monitors a patient having a nuclear stress test. Wilmington Health offers a full complement of cardiac testing services to its patients using state-of-the art equipment.

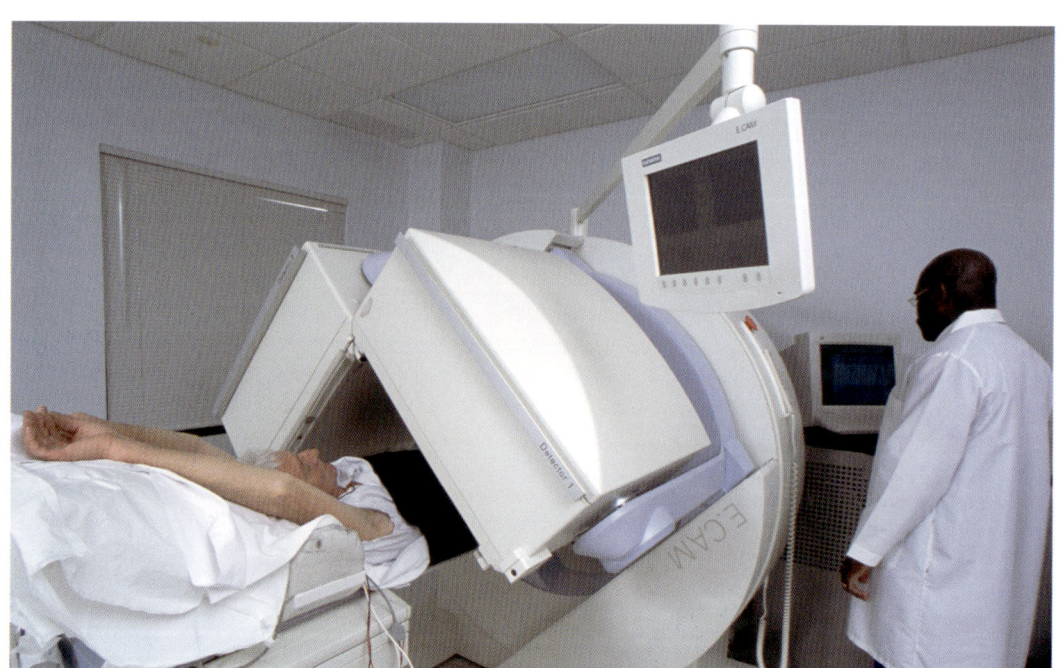

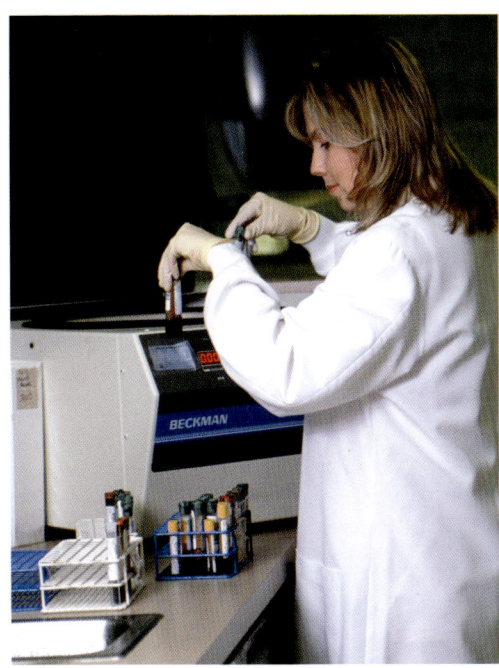

patients an opportunity to express concerns, ask questions or make suggestions regarding the practices' services and facilities.

The Patient Advisory Council has been instrumental in the development of a patient satisfaction questionnaire, many facility improvements including a bus stop at the main building, golf cart service to assist elderly or infirm patients from their cars, and additional handicap parking spaces. The council was also very instrumental in the adoption of the group's financial policy, according to Dr. Gottovi.

Each of the various divisions and locations of Wilmington Health offers the latest technology and equipment and each physician is highly trained in his or her field. Frequent meetings, workshops and retreats ensure focus and productivity, as well as promoting employee and physician morale. A large number of physicians remain involved in clinical research trials, as well as teaching and training of medical students.

In addition to providing the finest health services for its patients, Wilmington Health is committed to giving back to the community. The governing board established an annual charitable fund that it has used to donate funds to organizations such as the Domestic Violence Shelter, United Way, Brigade Boys and Girls Clubs, The Yahweh Center and numerous others. In 2004 the group co-sponsored the building of a home for Habitat for Humanity.

"Since we were founded in 1971, Wilmington Health Associates' mission has been to continually improve the quality of medical care to each of our patients. Doing what is right for the patient has always been our number one priority and this philosophy will continue to guide us in the future," says Dr. Gottovi.

For additional information and a complete listing of offices and services, please visit www.wilmingtonhealth.com.

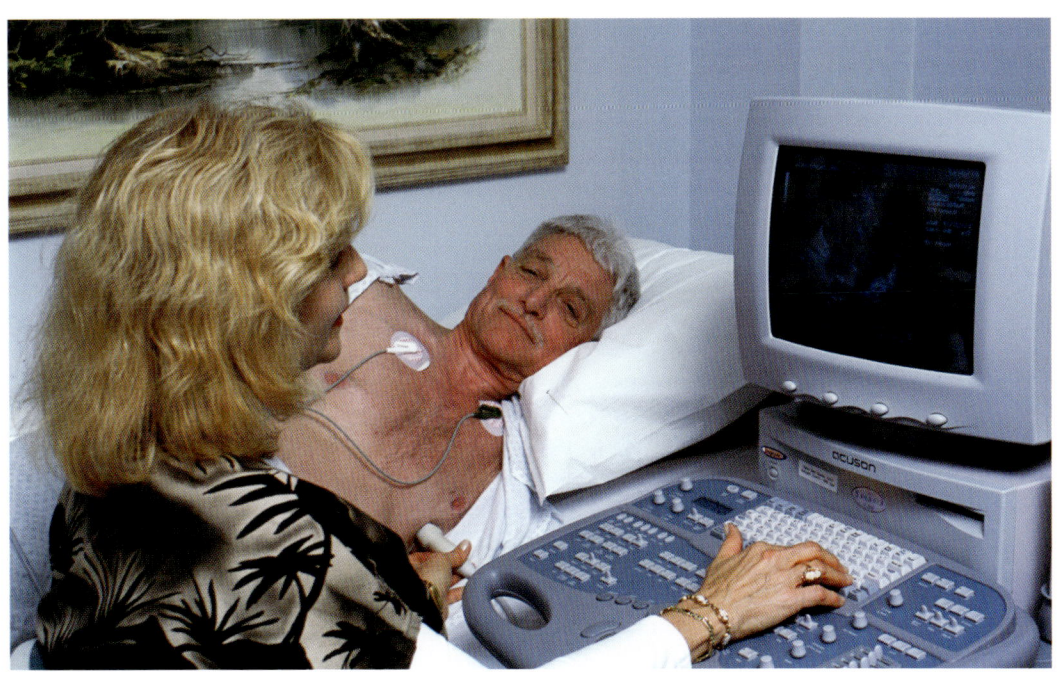

✧

Top: A lab technician prepares a patient's lab results. The main lab located at 1202 Medical Center Drive is CLIA certified and uses the most current, state-of-the art equipment. Wilmington Health also offers lab services at its satellite offices for patient convenience.

Bottom: A certified technician performs an echocardiogram on a patient, showing the heart's size, shape and movement. This is one of many tests that help physicians better diagnose and treat heart conditions.

Cape Fear Community College

The history of Cape Fear Community College began in 1958 when the North Carolina legislature approved a bold new venture in business and technical education. The legislature agreed to help communities establish trade and technical schools to train adults and selected high school students for careers in business and industry.

Wilmington was selected as one of the six original locations for an area technical school and the Wilmington Industrial Center opened in 1959. This small school, operating in one building and serving 750 students in its first year, has evolved into a leader in workforce training with more than sixty programs serving more than 25,000 residents of the greater Wilmington area each year.

Wilmington Industrial Education Center became Cape Fear Technical Institute in 1964 and evolved into Cape Fear Community College in 1988. The college's name reflects the vast Cape Fear coastal region of North Carolina and the school's main campus fronts on the beautiful Cape Fear River.

Cape Fear Community College offers extensive programs with concentrations in engineering and manufacturing technologies, business technologies, construction and transportation technologies, health sciences, college transfer/university parallel, law enforcement and other public services. The school's unique riverfront location and proximity to numerous beaches and natural estuaries account for the development of several specialized programs available, such as boat building, outboard/inboard marine systems and marine technology.

Today the college boasts more than sixty different curriculums as well as continuing education programs conducted at its Wilmington campus, three satellite campuses in northern New Hanover County, Hampstead and Burgaw, and scores of other locations throughout New Hanover and Pender Counties.

Cape Fear Community College's growth has been little short of phenomenal. The school's first building at Thirteenth and Market Streets in Wilmington was built with money supplied as part of a local bond issue. The thirty-two-thousand-square-foot facility included shop areas, classrooms, chemistry laboratory, physics laboratory, library and a small administrative office.

The Industrial Center, as it was then known, offered courses for high school students during the day and adults at night. Among the courses offered were radio and television service, heating and air conditioning service, internal combustion engine mechanics and draftsmanship. In addition, short-term pre-employment courses

were provided at new or expanding industrial establishments for new employees; and upgrading courses were provided for current employees.

The school was an immediate success and more than 750 adults and high school students received training the very first year. Interest continued at such a high level that it soon became obvious that high school and adult training would need to be separated if either was to receive adequate attention.

This problem was solved in 1963 when the legislature approved the Community College Act. Under provisions of the legislation, high school training remained as part of the public school system, while adult training of less than four-year college level became the responsibility of the Department of Community Colleges. Wilmington Industrial Education Center became an adult training center in 1963 but continued to share facilities with the high school students.

The ongoing growth of the school made it obvious that larger quarters would be necessary to meet the area's needs. With strong support from local industry and civic organizations such as the Chamber of Commerce Committee of 100 and the Merchant's Association, a $575,000 bond issue was proposed to match federal funds for building new facilities. Voters approved the bond issue by a three-to-one margin. Passage of the bond issue assured adequate facilities for expanded programs and in 1964 the Industrial Center became the Cape Fear Technical Institute.

Additional state and local bond issue referendums in 1993, 1994, 1997 and 2000, plus other local support, provided more than $100 million for additional growth. The college has been able to more than double the acreage and instructional space at its Wilmington campus, and enlarged the facilities at the Burgaw campus by forty percent. One hundred forty-two acres were acquired for an additional campus in northern New Hanover County and a new 117,000 square-foot building on the North Campus resulted in a three-fold expansion of the school's instructional facilities over pre-1994 levels. A second North Campus building is scheduled to open in 2005.

SHARING THE HERITAGE

Because the school has something for everyone, more than 25,000 people take classes at CFCC each year. Students may train for a new career in one of the school's technical programs or earn a two-year college transfer degree in order to continue their education at a four-year institution. CFCC also offers a wide variety of adult education and continuing education classes for lifelong learning.

For students wanting to start a new career, CFCC offers sixty technical programs in a wide range of disciplines. These programs provide hands-on training, making students eligible for a job as soon as they graduate.

In CFCC's popular college transfer program, students may earn the first two years of a bachelor's degree at a fraction of the cost of attending a four-year college or university. Once they complete their two-year degree they may transfer to any four-year college or university in North Carolina.

Cape Fear Community College also offers hundreds of continuing education programs, some of which are provided without charge. Free programs include basic skills, adult literacy, GED preparation, job skills preparation, adult high school and English as a second language.

The growing community service course offerings include arts and crafts, kayaking, and motorcycle safety. The college's Center for Business offers low-cost classes in computer training, construction, foreign languages, leadership and management. In measuring the quality of its curriculum programs, CFCC has examined the success of its graduates and the satisfaction of employees. The results are impressive. Ninety-nine percent of CFCC graduates were employed one year after graduation. According to the most recent employer satisfaction survey, ninety-eight percent of employers were satisfied with the quality of the CFCC graduates they hired.

Many graduates must pass certification exams to be licensed in their field, and CFCC graduates have one of the highest pass rates among all community colleges

in the state. In fields such as Associate Degree Nursing, CFCC graduates must take the same licensure examinations to become Registered Nurses as do graduates of four-year nursing programs at senior colleges and universities. CFCC's nursing graduates have consistently recorded higher passing rates on these licensure exams than their four-year counterparts.

Recent pass rates include 100 percent in Dental Hygiene, Licensed Practical Nursing, Occupational Therapy Assistant and Radiography; ninety-five percent in Associate Degree Nursing; and ninty-three percent in Basic Law Enforcement Training.

Cape Fear Community College guarantees that if an employer of any CFCC graduate finds the employee does not have the skills needed to perform the job, CFCC will retrain the graduate at no cost, provided the graduate earned at least a "C" in the course, and allows the College to share the graduate's class attendance record with the employer. In the most recent survey, employers took no exceptions to the CFCC Graduate Guarantee.

The history of CCFC will continue to evolve at a significant pace as the institution positions itself for the future with this vision statement: "Cape Fear Community College: Building a future-oriented world-class workforce and a community of lifelong learners in partnership with regional businesses and agencies." Imagine the possibilities!

You may visit CFCC on the internet at www.cfcc.edu.

Bald Head Island

For most of its long history, Bald Head Island was a beautiful, but wild, semitropical paradise best known for Old Baldy, a lighthouse commissioned in 1817 by Thomas Jefferson. Situated at the mouth of the Cape Fear River, near Southport, the island is the last of North Carolina's great strand of barrier islands.

In addition to its maritime navigation role, Bald Head Island has been the site of military forts in both the Revolutionary War and Civil War, a supplier of cedar for pencils, a messenger-pigeon roost, a hideout for pirates, and a nesting place for loggerhead turtles.

Prior to the early 1980s, the secluded island was best known as a hunting and fishing paradise. The twelve-thousand-acre island had a small number of modest vacation homes, a golf course, and a few paved roads. Power was supplied by generators, water came from wells or cisterns, and septic tanks provided sewage treatment.

The transformation of Bald Head Island began in 1983 when the Mitchell family of Texas acquired the island and developed it as a low density, ecologically sensitive residential and resort community, without automobiles, hotels, high rises or malls. George Mitchell is the founder of Mitchell Energy and Development Corporation, one of the nation's largest producers of natural gas and oil, and developer of The Woodlands, an acclaimed planned community near Houston, Texas. Mitchell's sons, Kent and Mark, guided the development of Bald Head Island, incorporating their father's tradition of sensitive, tasteful development.

Although earlier developers deeded more than 10,000 acres of marshland, oceanfront, and maritime forest to the state, in perpetuity, as a wildlife refuge, the Mitchells carry out their own vision for the island, which includes a commitment to retain its ecological integrity. To this end, they helped establish the Bald Head Island Conservancy, which oversees the continuing protection of island wildlife and their natural habitats.

Development of the remaining 2,000 acres began with the infrastructure: a water and sewer system, phone service, roads, and ferry service between the island and Southport. A chapel was built, Old Baldy Lighthouse was restored, and the Smith Island Museum of History came into being. Gasoline-powered vehicles were phased out, leaving electric golf carts as the island's primary mode of transportation.

The island's developers, architects, and land planners revived the architectural style that characterized such historic coastal communities as Nantucket, Ocracoke and old Nag's Head. Cape Fear Station, the developer's final planned community on the island, takes its name from the original U.S. Lifesaving Station sited just north of the legendary Cape Fear, with streets and neighborhoods named for other historic lifesaving stations that dotted the North Carolina Coast in the late nineteenth and early twentieth centuries.

Spectacular natural surroundings provide opportunities for kayaking, bird watching or beachcombing; while man-made amenities include an eighteen-hole golf course, croquet greenswards, tennis courts, pools, as well as an oceanfront club with direct beach access. A ten-acre marina, home of the Bald Head Island Yacht Club, lies at the heart of Harbour Village, a picture postcard neighborhood of cottages, bed and breakfast inns, small shops, and casual restaurants. Permanent residences and vacation homes are situated in every island environment.

On Bald Head Island, visitors and residents alike enjoy a simpler, more tranquil way of life, knowing the island's environmental integrity, historic character, and abundance of natural treasures are a legacy that will be passed on to the next generation.

For additional information, please visit www.baldheadisland.com or call 800-234-1666.

❖

Above: Built in 1903 as residences for the Cape Fear Lighthouse keepers and their families, these historic cottages overlooking Cape Fear are listed in the National Register of Historic Places.

Below: On Bald Head Island, an eighteen hole top-rated golf course is sculpted from the natural contours of sand dunes, maritime forest and freshwater lagoons.
PHOTOS COURTESY OF BALD HEAD ISLAND LIMITED.

SECURITY SAVINGS BANK

Security Savings Bank began as Southport Building & Loan Association in the back corner of a downtown pharmacy in 1911 with starting capital of $6,200.

Today, Security Savings has nine branches in Brunswick and Randolph Counties and assets total nearly $302 million.

This steady growth is attributed to the firm's commitment to "Serve the people and serve them well." From a small, hometown building and loan, organized to provide members with funds for homebuilding, Security has evolved into a true community bank while adding services such as checking, money market accounts, alternative investment products, debit/credit cards and commercial real estate and consumer installment loans.

The organization meeting of the Southport Building & Loan Association was held October 11, 1911, in the law office of Cranmer and Davis. Authorization had been given for issuing 200 shares of stock at $100 per share but business began after only 62 shares were subscribed. This created the starting capital of $6,200.

M. C. Guthrie was elected the firm's first president, S. B. Northrop became vice president and D. I. (Doc) Watson was named secretary-treasurer.

Members of the original Board of Directors were J. N. Daniels, Dr. J. A. Dosher, Richard Dosher, and J. J. Garrett. The other charter members were J. J. Loughlin, William St. George, A. J. Robbins, W. J. Weeks, E. H. Cranmer, and Robert W. Davis.

Watson, who served as secretary-treasurer for many years, was a colorful character that kept the building and loan's records in one corner of his prescription department at Watson's Pharmacy located on Moore Street in the present-day Pharmacy restaurant.

The secretary-treasurer took his job very seriously and kept a close eye on the association's business affairs. In the early days, most of the building and loan accounts were built up through small weekly savings. For Doc, Saturday was the end of the week and those who were late in paying on their shares were assessed a penalty. It is a matter of record that Watson exacted those penalties without show of favoritism.

There are stories also of members who considered their accounts a sort of transient spending fund and sought to borrow from the accounts after a weekend of unwise spending. When they came to the drug store to seek financial relief, Doc would tell them, "Well, you ain't going to get it," thus encouraging the practice of uninterrupted thrift.

There are stories, too, of loans Doc made to depositors from his own funds when he knew they were in genuine economic distress.

Watson served as secretary-treasurer until 1933 when he turned over the responsibility to James Carr, one of the most beloved businessmen in the City of Southport's history.

When Carr became managing officer the association moved into offices in the Smith Building on Moore Street. The offices remained there until 1958 when the firm moved into a new location on Moore Street, sharing a new building with the U.S. Post

❖

Security Savings Banks' managing officers throughout its history.

D. I. Watson
1911-1933

James E. Carr
1933-1952

William P. Jorgensen
1952-1968

Douglas H. Hawes
1969-1989

Albert G. Trunnell, Jr.
1989-1999

Kenneth W. Mabe
1999-

Office. In 1975 the Southport branch office was moved to its present location at the corner of Howe and Moore Streets.

Despite the worldwide depression of the 1930s and World War II, Security Savings grew steadily through the '30s and '40s. Assets totaled $94,806 in 1935 and had grown to $115,657 by 1938. At the end of World War II, in 1945, assets totaled $193,978.

A review of the firm's records provides a glimpse of how difficult it was to conduct business in those days. A letter from the state insurance commissioner, written as the depression deepened in 1932, warns that building and loan associations "should not undertake to finance new loans at this time, nor should withdrawal requests be granted until sufficient funds are in hand to meet maturities."

The firm's annual report for 1942 notes, "We begin the new year with the entire world at war, a war not only between dictatorship and democracy, but between the forces of good and evil. So let us look first to our eternal God for strength and guidance in this hour of turmoil and distress. Then let each of us begin the year 1942 with a renewed pledge to constantly improve ourselves, so that we can make this a better community in which to live."

The optimism that followed the war is reflected in a report to the shareholders dated January 25, 1946. "Mortgage loans are slightly higher than last year and indications are that applications for loans will increase as all restrictions have been lifted on building," read the report.

The association's growth continued on into the 1950s and in 1955, Security Savings reached its first million-dollar mark in assets.

Several outstanding businessmen led the association during these years. Serving as president during the era were J. N. Daniels, S. B. Northrop, R. C. Daniel and H. T. St. George. James Carr served as managing officer until 1952.

The decade of the '60s was a period of rapid growth for the association as Brunswick County saw increased business development and growth in population. Assets doubled from $2,576,174 in 1960 to $4,768,176 in 1965. By 1970, Security's assets had grown to $7,348,637.

In an effort to serve all areas of Brunswick County, the association opened an office in Shallotte in 1964. The firm's emphasis continued to be on local thrift and local lending for the purchase and construction of homes, which resulted in a strong economic impact throughout Brunswick County.

The firm's name was changed to Security Savings and Loan in 1964, reflecting the decision to expand services outside the immediate Southport area. Leading the association's growth during this period was managing officer William P. Jorgensen.

The 1970s saw assets soar from $7,348,637 in 1970 to $15,629,863 in 1975 and to $30,785,007 in 1980. In 1974 an additional branch office was opened in a third Brunswick County community, Leland.

Two more branches were opened in the 1980s, Calabash in 1983 and Oak Island in 1986. Assets continued to climb, more than doubling to $66,270,877 in 1985.

Security passed the $100 million milestone in assets in 1988 and by 1990 assets totaled

✧

Above: Security Savings Bank's first home loan was for this house to H. L. Dosher in 1911. The house, in Southport, is now occupied by Bob and Jan Quinn.

Below: Security Savings Bank Sunset Beach branch office, 2001.

Security Savings Bank Operations Center, 2002.

$120,813,000. In 1995 that figure had reached $173,666,666.

In 1985, *National Thrift News*, a savings industry publication, listed Security among the most profitable savings and loans in the country.

The association's commitment to local mortgage lending and its strong balance sheet enabled Security to avoid the economic troubles that plagued many S & Ls during the 1980s following deregulation of the industry.

L. J. Hardee and W. E. Bellamy, Jr., served as president during this period, along with managing officer Douglas Hawes.

In 1994 the name was changed to Security Savings Bank when the firm became a state savings bank. The primary reason for this change was to identify the bank as one of the best managed, well capitalized savings institutions in North Carolina.

Security reached across the state to Randolph County in 1999 to merge with Randleman Savings Bank. This allowed Security to enter the growing Randolph County market and offer home equity and construction loans, an expanded range of CDs and checking accounts to customers of Randleman Savings Bank.

Like Security, Randleman Savings began as a building and loan association in 1905 and later became a state-chartered mutual savings bank.

The merger increased the assets of Security Savings to $209,584,653 in 1999. An additional office was opened in Sunset Beach in Brunswick County in 2001.

A merger with Liberty Savings and Loan Association in Randolph County in 2003 provided Security with an even larger profile in the state's booming Piedmont region. The latest merger increased total assets to $301,402,533.

Albert G. Trunnell, Jr. served as managing officer beginning in 1989 and in 1990, took on the title of president and CEO, guiding the bank during much of this growth period. He retired in 1999 and was succeeded by Kenneth W. Mabe, who has been with the bank since 1992. Trunnell was elected chairman of the bank's Board of Directors in 2004.

In addition to meeting the financial needs of the communities it serves, Security is deeply involved in community service projects.

A good example of this involvement is the bank's leadership in raising flood relief funds following disastrous hurricane Floyd in 1999. The bank started the Brunswick County Hurricane Relief Fund by challenging the Brunswick County Community Foundation to raise money for local relief and agreeing to match any funds raised up to $10,000. The campaign raised more than $30,000. Statewide, more than $805,000 was raised through the North Carolina Community Foundation for hurricane relief.

In addition, Security led a campaign to raise funds needed to rebuild the historic Southport Community Building, which was destroyed by fire in 1995. The facility served as a USO during World War II and in more recent times as a meeting place for civic clubs and a location for weddings, reunions, holiday events and cultural activities. Security's president and CEO Kenneth Mabe led the successful campaign, and the bank provided the construction financing.

Security Savings Bank's strategic plan envisions continued growth for the bank that started with only $6,200 in 1911. The plan says, "The primary driving force behind the bank continues to be to serve the banking needs of Brunswick and Randolph Counties, and remain a mutual savings bank."

Speaking to the bank's core values, the strategic plan notes, "Our reason for existing is to serve our customers. We are dedicated to the communities we live in and the customers we serve. We are a product of our community and a leader in our community. We take the needs of our community seriously and will take no action that may be harmful to our community."

LOWER CAPE FEAR HISTORICAL SOCIETY

When the Lower Cape Fear Historical Society was incorporated in 1956, there were 336 members. The goals of the Society were to publish a new history of the area, form archives, sponsor historic outings for the members, have regular speakers on local history, have an essay contest and awards for historical writings and work and lobby for identification and preservation of historic sites. After fifty years, nearly 800 members work together in the interests of history toward these goals.

The Bulletin, published three times a year, has covered topics of interest by scholarly authors touching nearly every part of Cape Fear History, from founding families to presiding judges. The first archives were house in a fireproof safe in the New Hanover County Courthouse. Now the archives and library are located in many file cabinets, shelves and boxes on the second floor of the Latimer House and include several unique collections donated by local historians.

Since 1963, when the Zebulon Latimer House was purchased by the Lower Cape Fear Historical Society, tours of that elegant Italianate mansion furnished in the ornate Victorian style have been an important part of the work of the Society. Volunteers tell the story of the Latimer family and their place in the history of Wilmington. It is the only historic home open to the public with so many furnishings original to the house's family.

Preservation concerns led to the support of a new organization to help preserve the bricks and mortar of this historic area and the Historic Wilmington Foundation was created forty years ago. Thanks to a memorial fund for noted local Historian, Louis T. Moore, the Society has published and reprinted numerous volumes about the history of the Cape Fear region.

Board members and members of the Society have led the organization in many directions including archeological digs at Old Town Plantation and the servants' quarters behind the Latimer House. Awards have been created to honor outstanding writing about local history and dedicated service to the Society and the community.

The Lower Cape Fear Historical Society has made a significant impact on this historic community and intends to continue "preserving and disseminating" information and knowledge.

❖

Top, left: Latimer House.

Top, right: Latimer House garden.

Bottom, left: Old Wilmington by Candlelight Tour.

Bottom, right: Children at Discover Wilmington! summer camp.

Wilmington Surgical Associates

For more than a half century, Wilmington Surgical Associates has provided patients with the finest technology in healthcare as well as a patient-doctor relationship that emphasizes personal attention. The doctors at Wilmington Surgical Associates are dedicated to a philosophy that combines the old-fashioned doctor-patient relationship with world-class surgical skill.

Wilmington Surgical Associates was established in 1951 when Wilmington physician R. Bertram Williams, Jr., M.D., FACS, opened a medical practice in his boyhood home on North Third Street. Dr. Williams received his medical training at the University of North Carolina and Vanderbilt University and had a special interest in general and endocrine surgery. Dr. Williams also founded the New Hanover Health Network Foundation, which has been instrumental in providing support for healthcare in the community.

Horace G. Moore Jr., M.D., FACS, joined Dr. Williams in 1958 after completing his training at Johns Hopkins and the University of Washington with special expertise in gastric surgery.

Ellis A. Tinsley, Sr., M.D., FACS, came into the partnership in 1967 after completing his training at Vanderbilt University Hospitals and School of Medicine. Dr. Tinsley performed Wilmington's first pacemaker implantation in the late 1960s and initiated the use of carotid arteriography and carotid endarterectomy, a procedure that reduces the risk of stroke from atherosclerosis involving the carotid arterial wall. As the first board-certified thoracic surgeon in southeastern North Carolina, Dr. Tinsley introduced new treatments for lung cancer to the community. In 1990, he performed the first laparoscopic gall bladder procedure in southeastern North Carolina. The North Carolina Chapter of the American College of Surgeons honored him in 2003 as the "Surgeon of the Year."

The partnership evolved into Wilmington Surgical Associates, P.A., in 1973 when the practice moved to 1414 Medical Center Drive. This association allowed the practice to focus on providing the latest techniques in general, laparoscopic, oncologic, pediatric, thoracic, and vascular surgery to the patients of southeastern North Carolina. The group continues the tradition of medical pioneering established by its founders.

Ellis A. Tinsley, Jr., M.D., FACS, joined the practice in 1993 after completing a vascular surgery fellowship at the University of North Carolina Hospitals. Dr. Tinsley holds board certification in both general and vascular surgery and has introduced minimally invasive techniques in vascular surgery including overnight stay for carotid endarterectomy, small incision in-situ bypass, and endovascular aneurysm repair. With a broad interest in surgery, he performed the first laparoscopic hernia repair and laparoscopic splenectomy in the group. In addition to vascular and laparocopic surgery, Dr. Tinsley performs general, breast, vascular, thoracic and pediatric surgery. He continues to advocate for the patient at the bedside.

Although each physician at Wilmington Surgical Associates is trained in all aspects of general surgery, the practice has developed three centers of excellence. The Vascular Center, The Heartburn Center, and The Breast Center are located at the practice's offices at 1414 Medical Center Drive.

The Heartburn Center provides verification for heartburn and screens candidates for minimally invasive surgery. The Breast Center provides advanced procedures that greatly reduce the amount of time a patient must wait for biopsy results. The Vascular Center focuses on noninvasive diagnostic testing for patients at risk for stroke, poor circulation, or aneurysm and their follow-up.

The Heartburn Center provides quality, comprehensive services for patients with

❖

The original physician group at Wilmington Surgical Associates (from left to right):
Dr. Horace G. Moore, Jr.,
Dr. Ellis A. Tinsley, Sr., and
Dr. R. Bertram Williams, Jr.

gastroesophageal reflux disease, commonly referred to as GERD. Chronic heartburn sufferers are offered state-of-the-art diagnostic tests and procedures that offer patients freedom from the dependence on drugs prescribed by traditional GERD treatment.

Mark F. Medley, M.D., director of The Heartburn Center, joined Wilmington Surgical Associates in 1995 after completing his training at Tulane Medical Center and a fellowship in laparoscopic surgery at Georgia Baptist Hospital in Atlanta. Dr. Medley added to the practices' reputation for innovation by introducing laparoscopic removal of the spleen and adrenal glands. He has performed many laparoscopic gallbladder surgeries with instruments as small as two millimeters. In addition to his concentration on advanced laparoscopic surgery, Dr. Medley performs general, breast, vascular, thoracic, and pediatric surgery.

Gregory G. Bebb, M.D., who directs The Breast Center, joined the practice in 1997 following a three-year fellowship at the City of Hope comprehensive Cancer Center in California. A surgical oncologist, Dr. Bebb has introduced sentinel lymph node mapping, a technique for tracking the spread of invasive melanoma. This technique gives the patient proportionately better odds for timely, effective treatment.

Dr. Bebb also introduced office-based ultrasound-guided needle core biopsy for the detection of breast cancer. This innovative diagnostic procedure greatly decreases the amount of time a patient must wait for results. The maximum time lapse for this procedure is about forty-eight hours, much better than the weeks of "wait-and-worry" involved with traditional testing procedures.

Robert Cortina, M.D., joined Wilmington Surgical Associates in 2001 after completing a Cardiothoracic Fellowship at the University of Rochester. He has been instrumental in developing Wilmington's first multidisciplinary thoracic oncology clinic. He also performs numerous complex operations using minimally invasive surgical techniques for both benign and malignant disease.

The medical director for The Vascular Center is Thomas David Eskew, Jr., M.D. Dr. Eskew is a vascular surgeon who completed his fellowship training at Kansas University Medical Center in Kansas City, Kansas, and an endovascular fellowship at Southern Illinois University in Springfield. Board certified in both vascular and general surgery, he pioneered endovascular techniques in vascular surgery for arteries and veins.

James R. Morgan, M.S., R.V.T. is technical director for The Vascular Center. He is past president of the North Carolina Society of Vascular Technology and on the ultrasound faculty of the Bowman Gray School of Medicine.

The Vascular Center was one of the first forty noninvasive vascular laboratories in the nation to be accredited by the Intersocietal Commission for the Accreditation of Vascular Laboratories. Over four thousand noninvasive vascular studies are performed each year.

After more than fifty years, the highly skilled surgeons, medical professionals and staff at Wilmington Surgical Associates remain dedicated to providing meaningful patient-doctor relationships that restore, comfort and encourage.

✧

Top, left: The original offices of Wilmington Surgical Associates at 1414 Medical Center Drive in Wilmington.

Top, right: The current offices of Wilmington Surgical Associates at 1414 Medical Center Drive in Wilmington.

Below: The current physician group at Wilminton Surgical Associates. Back row (from left to right): Dr. Gregory G. Bebb, Dr. Mark F. Medley, and Dr. Ellis A Tinsley, Jr. Front row (from left to right): Dr. Robert M. Cortina, and Dr. Thomas D. Eskew, Jr.

Z.A. Sneeden

Z.A. Sneeden founded his grading and utility contracting company in 1910, based on a foundation that his word was his bond. He maintained a belief in free enterprise and wanted to establish himself as a sound businessman.

His first office was combined with a shop and equipment on Oleander Drive near Seagate. From the onset of the Depression until 1945, the office was located in the Odd Fellow's Building at Third and Princess Streets. Sneeden constructed an office building at Sixteenth and Wooster Streets in 1945. During his first year of business he employed a dozen people, paying the average wage of a dollar a day; mules and pans were the equipment of the time.

One of the firm's early contracts was for building the first streets on Wrightsville Beach. Sneeden used the mules and pans to grade present-day Lumina Avenue from Station One north. Since there was no vehicular bridge connecting Wrightsville, mules and equipment were transported in boxcars by Tide Water Power Company, operator of the trolley to the beach. The firm graded other streets at Wrightsville in Wilmington, and throughout the state. When Dow Chemical Company moved to Wilmington in the 1930's, Sneeden obtained a grading contract with the corporation, which was a major job during the Depression. During the post-World War II years, Sneeden became actively involved as a grading and utilities contractor due to the construction of Camp Davis, Camp Lejeune, and the Wilmington Shipyard. The paving industry was developing at that time, also.

❖

Z.A. Sneeden, founder of Z.A. Sneeden's Sons, Inc.

Sneeden instilled in his sons his pioneer spirit, and upon completion of their military service, he encouraged their business interest and began giving them stock in the company. After the demise of Z. A. Sneeden in 1951, his four sons—Jack A., E. B., D. W., and T. W.—continued the firm's operation.

During the late 1950s and early '60s the sons divided responsibilities and established separate enterprises. T. W. Sneeden and E. B. Sneeden opened Hanover Company and deal mainly with grading and paving. D. W. Sneeden established Lincoln Construction Company, a heavy-grading business. Jack A. Sneeden continued to operate Z. A. Sneeden's Sons, Inc. where he emulated his father's pioneer liveliness in his business expertise.

In the 1960s, Z. A. Sneeden's Sons, under Jack A. Sneeden as president, became a commercial developing company in North Carolina. These included several

strip malls, office buildings, Southern Bell Centers, and restaurant franchises.

Jack A. Sneeden's interests were not limited to his business; he served on the board of trustees of Meredith College in Raleigh for nearly twenty years. His religious involvement included serving on the board of deacons and holding various offices of the First Baptist Church of Wilmington. He also served on various other charitable organizations.

Upon his death in 1985, Elnora G. Sneeden became president. The Sneeden children have joined the company and are well into the third generation. Today the company does commercial building and developing.

SHARING THE HERITAGE

Brunswick Community College

"Celebrating Twenty-five Years of Community Involvement...With You, For You, Because of You."

Brunswick Community College traces its beginnings to 1977 when civic leader Bobbie Varnam and Brunswick County Commissioner William "Bill" Stanley led a drive to secure signatures on a petition urging creation of a college in Brunswick County. This resulted in a feasibility study by the North Carolina Department of Community Colleges and the formation of Brunswick Technical Institute in May 1979. The legislative bill established the new school, which was introduced by Representative Tom Rabon. The county then deeded a building to the school, which is located near the intersections of U.S. 17 and U.S. 211 in Supply.

The Board of Trustees, installed in September 1979, hired the school's first employee; Barbara Reaves, in December 1979 and Brunswick County native Dr. Joseph Carter became the college's first president in February 1980.

Brunswick Technical Institute opened its doors in 1980 with nearly 100 curriculum students and 2,400 students in continuing education classes. The first student to enroll was twenty-one-year old Michael Hankins of Sunset Harbor. The first graduation was held in 1981 with 10 students receiving diplomas in welding, one each in light construction and auto mechanics, and 31 students receiving general education (GED) diplomas. In 2003, BCC served over 1,100 curriculum and 7,500 continuing education students.

The school's name was changed to Brunswick Technical College in October 1979. Eight years later, in 1987, the Board of Trustees and the Brunswick County Board of Commissioners approved a name change they felt would reflect the school's ultimate identity—Brunswick Community College.

The gift of the former Brunswick Training Center in Southport from the Brunswick County Board of Education doubled the college's size in 1981. Added programs were: Cosmetology, Automotive, Nursing Assistant, Practical Nursing Education, and Air Conditioning, Heating and Refrigeration.

The Brunswick Interagency Program was established in 1983 as a way to offer a comprehensive work-training educational program for adults with physical or mental disabilities. This program now serves 125 students. Also in 1983, the first permanent building at the BCC site in Supply was completed. It contained bays for Welding, Automotive Mechanics, and Air Conditioning, Heating and Refrigeration.

In 1985, Brunswick County voters, by a margin of three to one, endorsed the school's accomplishments and approved an $8-million bond for construction on the main campus. At the time, this was the largest bond referendum amount ever sought by a North Carolina community college.

The Small Business Center, funded by a state grant in 1986, was designed to meet the needs of small businesses and entrepreneurs. That endeavor expanded in 1997 to include a Business Incubator Center in Winnabow, which provides space at a low cost to help small businesses become established. The

✧

Above: W. Michael Reaves, Ed.D. president of Brunswick Community College.

Below: Brunswick Community College's first graduating class in 1981. Ten students received diplomas in welding, one in light construction and one in auto mechanics.

incubator was a joint collaboration of BCC, Brunswick County Economic Development Corporation and Rural Consumer Services Corporation, a subsidiary of Brunswick Electric Membership Corporation.

Dr. W. Michael Reaves became the school's second president in 1988 placing an emphasis on cooperation with other Brunswick county agencies. His immediate goal was to complete the $8 million bond construction project, then add curriculum programs to meet the unique needs of Brunswick County residents.

A new technical classroom building was completed in 1988 and the nursing and cosmetology departments joined the business and general education programs in Supply. The Administration/Library/Student Services building was completed in 1989.

In 1990, BCC entered into a collaborative agreement with the University of North Carolina at Wilmington allowing BCC students to transfer to university programs as juniors. Currently, BCC has Comprehensive Articulation Agreements with the sixteen University of North Carolina campuses for students completing the Associate of Arts or Science degrees. Also in 1990, the Brunswick County Commissioners appropriated $1.1 million to build a center in the Leland Industrial Park for training and assistance for businesses. That center also houses the Basic Law Enforcement Training program, Brunswick Interagency Program, nursing, computer, and curriculum classes.

The college has offered dual enrollment for high school students since 1980 and, in 1991, the technical and vocational "Tech Prep" program was designed to offer technical courses to high school students.

BCC joined the Eastern Carolina Community College Athletic Conference in 1991 and established a golf team that year. The men's basketball program began in 1995 and won the Region 10 Carolinas Conference of the National Junior College Athletic Association in 2005.

Construction of the BCC Odell Williamson Auditorium in 1993 provided the county a fifteen-hundred-seat state-of-the-art facility for performing arts events as well as space for school, organization, and business activities and special events for county residents.

In 1995 the College established the College Transfer program and received a grant for the North Carolina Information Highway system so distance learning, Internet-based courses and telecourses could be offered.

A generous donation from LaDane Williamson in 1998 created scholarships of $1,200 each for recent Brunswick County high school or GED graduates not qualifying for Federal Pell grants.

A new Science and Health Education Building with thirteen classrooms and eight labs lab was completed in 1999. Also in 1999 the College established a visiting scholars program. Under this program, scholars from throughout the world have visited the College and brought their world perspectives to students, staff and the community.

In 2000, The Center for Aquaculture Technology complex was constructed, which includes an eighty-three-hundred-square-foot building and houses tank rooms, a hatchery and an indoor re-circulating culture system. Twenty outdoor ponds complete the complex.

Responding to the needs of the growing Hispanic community in Brunswick County, in 2004 the College entered into an agreement with Brunswick County Public Schools and the Mexican government to establish the Brunswick Educational Transition Center. This center helps children and adults learn English, become acclimated to American Culture, and expand their skills.

The growth of Brunswick Community College fostered the passing of a $30-million bond referendum in 2004. Planned construction includes an Applied Plant Sciences Facility, Student Center, three Continuing Education Centers, an Early Childhood Education Center, and a multipurpose Athletic and Community Center.

✧

Above: In 1983 the first permanent building at the new BCC Supply campus housed Welding, Automotive Mechanics, and Air Conditioning, Heating and Refrigeration.

Below: Bobbie Varnam started the process to create a Community College in Burnswick County in 1977.

SHARING THE HERITAGE

New Hanover Health Network

On June 14, 1967, seven prematurely born infants arrived in cardboard cradles as tiny ambassadors in perhaps the crowning civil rights achievement in the history of Wilmington, North Carolina.

They were the first patients of the newly opened New Hanover Memorial Hospital. During a turbulent period of civil rights in this nation's history, their arrival marked the merger, in a small city in the Deep South, of black and white hospitals—without protest, riot or bloodshed. For the first time, the county's hospital treated everyone, regardless of race, creed, national origin or ability to pay.

But the opening of what is today known as New Hanover Regional Medical Center was not without difficulty and controversy, a trait it shares with the overall history of health and healing in southeastern North Carolina. That history, also marked by outstanding achievement and innovation, is as much about war, politics, race relations, philanthropy, and public sanitation as it is about doctors and medicine.

Wilmington boasts the state's first licensed medical doctor, Armand DeRosset; the state's first African-American licensed M.D., Francis Shober; and one of the state's first medical and nursing schools. Dr. Thomas Fanning Wood and Dr. Moses John DeRosset III, the founders of public health in the state, are from Wilmington. And one of the state's earliest and most innovative specialty hospitals, Babies Hospital, cared for children in the salt air of nearby Wrightsville Beach under the direction of Dr. J. Buren Sidbury.

But the region's first hospitals had one of two functions: caring for the sick and wounded from the battlefield or caring for ailing sailors returning from sea.

As was the case with many of the early hospitals, the region's first was seized rather than built. British soldiers during the Revolutionary War commandeered St. James Church in downtown Wilmington to care primarily for soldiers who had fallen ill. During the Civil War, the same story was often repeated as armies from both sides confiscated buildings for temporary use as hospitals. The concern over the spread of infectious disease, usually via unsanitary conditions, worried military leaders far more than actual battlefield injury. A deadly yellow fever epidemic in 1862 in Wilmington helped confirm their fears of cities as havens for plagues and disease.

By 1857 a major railway had connected Wilmington to Virginia. Wilmington had grown into the state's largest city and cultural center. The federal government commissioned a hospital and hired Scottish builder James Walker to build it. The construction of U.S. Marine Hospital cost $43,898. Walker stayed in Wilmington and in 1900 commissioned the construction of a new hospital in his adopted hometown.

James Walker Memorial Hospital was a state-of-the-art hospital when it opened in 1902. It

✧
COURTESY OF THE CAPE FEAR MUSEUM, WILMINGTON, NORTH CAROLINA.

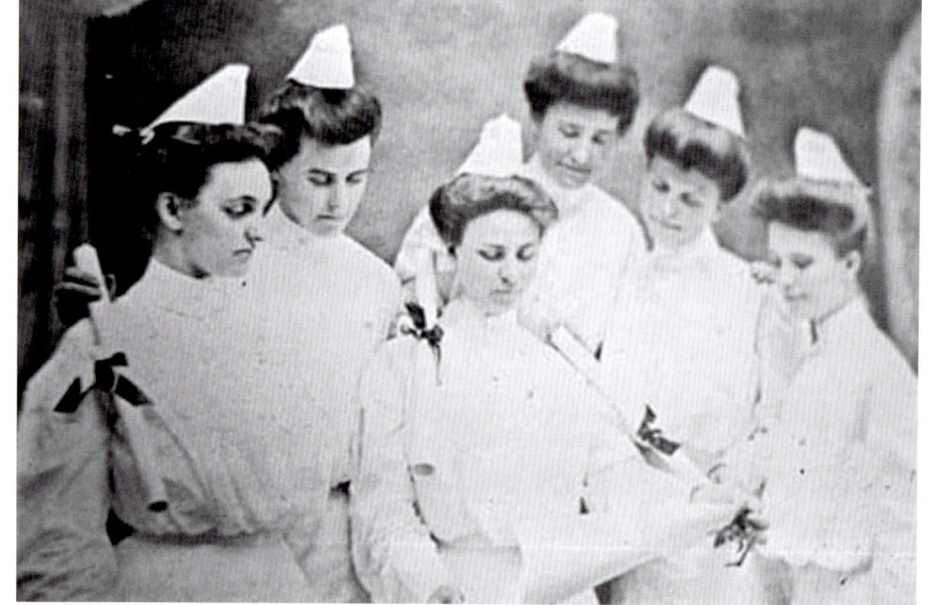

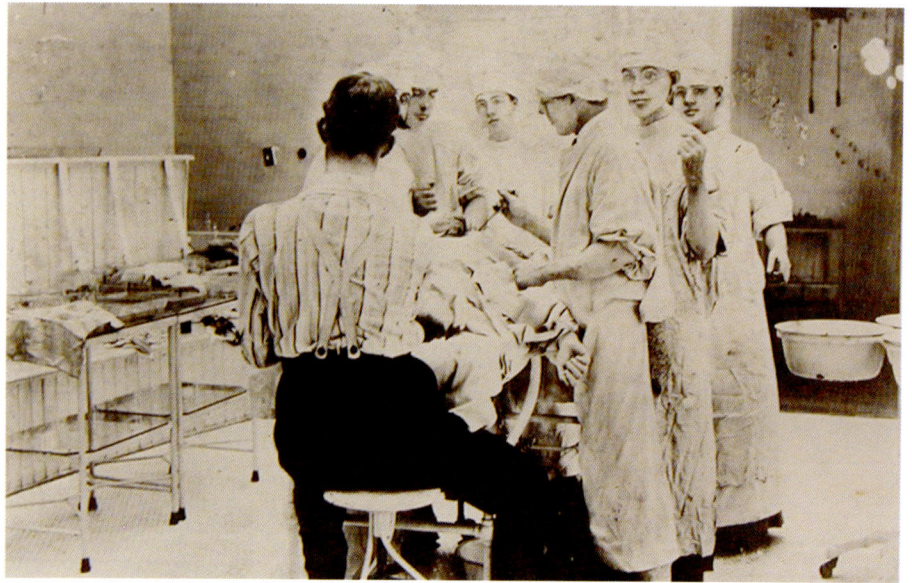

opened a nursing school for registered nurses and featured a women's unit and horse drawn ambulance service. It also had a "colored annex," but it was clear that, in a town torn by a racial riot in 1898, access to care was not equal. African-American physicians, disgusted by their inability to practice, opened Community Hospital and a nursing school in 1921. The two hospitals operated separately for the next forty-six years.

By 1947, James Walker Hospital had become outdated. The hospital board asked the county for funds to rebuild, but the issue died for lack of interest. In 1953 the James Walker board again asked for public money to build a new hospital, and again the proposal failed. Four years later, three prominent physicians pooled their resources and opened the private Cape Fear Memorial Hospital. But that did not solve the problem of the major hospital facility being outdated.

With the area's physicians saying current facilities were obsolete, there was enough interest in 1958 for voters to decide whether to build a new hospital. It failed by a 2-to-1 margin. Supporters of a new hospital rallied again for another bond vote, but encountered opposition from African-American leaders who didn't trust the white community to build an integrated hospital. Leaders of the drive for a new hospital tirelessly courted the black community, as well as the community at large, to support the proposed hospital.

Another vote was held on November 7, 1961. With all votes tallied except one precinct—a mostly black downtown precinct—the "no" votes led the ballot. But by then, a foundation of trust had been built. The last precinct came in overwhelmingly in favor of the hospital and the referendum passed.

Less than six years later, New Hanover Memorial Hospital opened the same day James Walker Memorial Hospital closed. The first patients were prematurely born infants, and they arrived in a caravan of ambulances who traveled a route prescribed by law enforcement from throughout the region. The region had come together as one healthcare community for the first time.

Today, New Hanover Health Network includes three hospital campuses and is

licensed for 855 beds. New Hanover Regional Medical Center is the primary referral hospital in the region, with specialty centers in cardiac, cancer, obstetrics, trauma, vascular surgery, intensive care, rehabilitation, and psychiatry. In 1998, New Hanover Regional and Cape Fear Hospital merged. Cape Fear now operates an orthopedic specialty center. The medical center manages Pender Memorial Hospital, serving residents in the county north of New Hanover.

The network acquired the county's emergency medical services in 1998 and added the region's first air ambulance service in 2001, around the same time it took a national lead in disaster response planning. One year later, New Hanover Regional EMS became the state's first model EMS system.

A freestanding cancer center opened in 2001, and two years later the cancer program was designated a national Teaching Hospital Program by the American College of Surgeons' Commission on Cancer.

In 2003 the American Nurses Association designated New Hanover Regional, including the Cape Fear campus, as the seventieth Nursing Magnet Hospital in the world. In 2004, New Hanover Regional was proposing a major expansion project that would establish a standalone women's and children's hospital and a surgery pavilion—all next to the original tower that quietly ushered in an era of health and racial equality four decades before.

Plantation Village

In 1962, Champion McDowell Davis, a local railroad executive, planted eighty-three thousand pine seedlings on Porters Neck Plantation. Thus creating a land use plan designed to provide residential, recreation, and healthcare oppor-tunities on his plantation.

✧

Above: Plantation Village is located at 1200 Porters Neck Road in Wilmington, and on the Internet at www.plantationvillagerc.com.

Below: Books are available at the library for residents to enjoy. The library is just one of the many amenities offered at Plantation Village.

In 1988, when the pine seedlings were matured, Plantation Village, as a part of Davis' land use plan, opened as the area's only continuing care retirement community.

Today, Plantation Village encompasses fifty-six acres on Porters Neck Plantation. The focal point of the acreage is the lovely blue Heron Pond, which is surrounded by dogwoods, wisteria, magnolias and more than fifteen hundred azaleas. Built around the pond are 190 independent living homes ranging from one- and two-bedroom apartments to large duplex homes with attached garages.

The serene setting, only minutes from downtown Wilmington and the popular Wrightsville Beach, offers five miles of walking trails weaving through the wooden areas, past lush plantings and over the footbridges which cross the pond.

Enjoying such a lovely setting, residents are involved with many planned activities. For exercise there's Tai Chi, line dancing, yoga and water aerobics in an enclosed pool. The well-equipped gym offers an opportunity to stay physically fit. Painting classes, computer classes, book clubs and lectures are just a few of the weekly activities. Community golfers appreciate discounted privileges at the neighborhood Porters Neck Country Club course.

Delicious chef-prepared meals are enjoyed in the Magnolia Room, a lovely country club style restaurant. This setting provides residents one of the social highlights of the day.

A full service community, Plantation Village offers the convenience of weekly housekeeping, linen service, indoor and outdoor maintenance and grounds keeping. Appliances are furnished in each home and utilities and cable are a part of the monthly service package.

As a continuing care community, Plantation Village offers two unique benefits. A Resident Care Center, staffed with licensed nurses twenty-four hours a day, provide services such as emergency response, routine blood pressure checks, vital sign monitoring and consultations. In-home services are provided as needed.

Should a resident no longer be capable of independent living, guaranteed access to Champions at Porters Neck Assisted Living and the Davis Health Care Center is available. Both healthcare facilities are located next door to Plantation Village.

Presenting a sound financial investment, Plantation Village's Return-of-Capital Plan offers a ninety percent refund of entrance fees to residents or to their estate without regard to length of residency. The plan allows retirees to make decisions for today, as well as protect their assets for the future.

Plantation Village is the only retirement community in the Wilmington area managed by Life Care Services, the industry leader with more than forty years of experience in more than one hundred senior communities across the nation. Life Care Services has managed Plantation Village since its inception, providing a guarantee of stability, both now and for the future.

WILMINGTON DEVELOPMENT CO., INC.

When Horace "Whitey" Prevatte hitchhiked from his home in Bladen County to Wilmington he had a head full of dreams and five dollars in his pocket. Today, Prevatte's Wilmington Development Co. operates successful restaurants, hotels and a shopping center. In addition, Whitey was instrumental in the development of the Battleship North Carolina Memorial.

Whitey, who learned to cook in the Army, started his career earning eighteen dollars a week to cook at the Jiffy Grill in 1948. He then became a dining car steward on the Atlantic Coastline Railway passenger train that made a daily run from New York to Miami.

That career came to an abrupt end in 1953 when the train crashed near Dillon, South Carolina, killing nine persons. Whitey escaped without a scratch but decided to find a safer way to make a living.

He had managed to save $1,200 from his railroad job and the Mayor of Wilmington at the time, "Red" Allsbrook, agreed to lend the ambitious restaurateur $1,339. "My mother-in-law loaned another $400 and Swift & Co. and some other suppliers gave me thirty days credit and I was in business," Whitey explains.

The El-Berta Restaurant, located next to the El Berta Motor Inn at 4501 Market Street opened on June 28, 1954. "We took in fifty-five dollars the first day and I was determined to make the restaurant a success," Whitey says. Since the restaurant was open twenty-four hours a day that often meant twenty-hour days for Whitey.

The delicious food and friendly service caught on and by the early '60s, Whitey was able to expand the restaurant and branch out into the catering business.

Whitey's next business venture came in 1966 when he bought twelve acres at Market and Kerr Avenue, then the site of an old sawmill, Cape Fear Lumber Company. Whitey and a partner, Dr. Heber Johnson, developed the Market Plaza Shopping Center on the site and today the busy center is home to twenty stores.

Whitey purchased the eighty-one room El Berta Motor Inn in 1975 and added a Sleep Inn Motel at 5225 Market Street in 1997. The Main Stay Suites, with sixty-three suites at 5229 Market Street in 2003, followed this.

Along the way, Whitey acquired 112 acres along Highway 421 and part of this property became the site for the Battleship North Carolina Memorial. Fifty-two acres of that property was donated in 2003 to the New Hanover County Soil and Water Conservation group.

Whitey acquired Dr. Johnson's interest in the shopping center in the late '80s and merged the restaurants and shopping center into Wilmington Development Co., Inc. in 1993.

The enterprise now employs about eighty people and is headquartered in the El Berta Motor Inn. Four employees at Whitey's Restaurant, Liz Fancher, Linda Rodgers, Phyllis Cox and Cora Hollis have been with the firm more than thirty years. Another employee, Patsy McKoy, retired after thirty years.

Whitey's two sons, Michael and Brian, grew up in the restaurant/hotel business and now serve as executives in the corporation.

✧

Top: Whitey Prevatte outside Whitey's Restaurant at 4501 Market Street.

Below: Whitey with his four employees who have worked at Whitey's Restaurant for over thirty years. Left to Right: Phyllis Cox, Cora Hollis, Liz Fancher and Linda Rodgers.

SHARING THE HERITAGE

For more information about the following publications or about publishing your own book, please call
Historical Publishing Network at 800-749-9790 or visit www.lammertinc.com.

Black Gold: The Story of Texas Oil & Gas

Historic Abilene: An Illustrated History

Historic Amarillo: An Illustrated History

Historic Anchorage: An Illustrated History

Historic Austin: An Illustrated History

Historic Baton Rouge: An Illustrated History

Historic Beaufort County: An Illustrated History

Historic Beaumont: An Illustrated History

Historic Bexar County: An Illustrated History

Historic Brazoria County: An Illustrated History

Historic Charlotte:
An Illustrated History of Charlotte and Mecklenburg County

Historic Cheyenne: A History of the Magic City

Historic Comal County: An Illustrated History

Historic Corpus Christi: An Illustrated History

Historic Denton County: An Illustrated History

Historic Edmond: An Illustrated History

Historic El Paso: An Illustrated History

Historic Erie County: An Illustrated History

Historic Fairbanks: An Illustrated History

Historic Gainesville & Hall County: An Illustrated History

Historic Gregg County: An Illustrated History

Historic Hampton Roads: Where America Began

Historic Henry County: An Illustrated History

Historic Houston: An Illustrated History

Historic Illinois: An Illustrated History

Historic Kern County:
An Illustrated History of Bakersfield and Kern County

Historic Laredo:
An Illustrated History of Laredo & Webb County

Historic Louisiana: An Illustrated History

Historic Midland: An Illustrated History

Historic Montgomery County:
An Illustrated History of Montgomery County, Texas

Historic Oklahoma: An Illustrated History

Historic Oklahoma County: An Illustrated History

Historic Omaha:
An Illustrated History of Omaha and Douglas County

Historic Pasadena: An Illustrated History

Historic Passaic County: An Illustrated History

Historic Philadelphia: An Illustrated History

Historic Prescott:
An Illustrated History of Prescott & Yavapai County

Historic Richardson: An Illustrated History

Historic Rio Grande Valley: An Illustrated History

Historic Scottsdale: A Life from the Land

Historic Shreveport-Bossier:
An Illustrated History of Shreveport & Bossier City

Historic South Carolina: An Illustrated History

Historic Smith County: An Illustrated History

Historic Texas: An Illustrated History

Historic Victoria: An Illustrated History

Historic Tulsa: An Illustrated History

Historic Williamson County: An Illustrated History

Iron, Wood & Water: An Illustrated History of Lake Oswego

Miami's Historic Neighborhoods: A History of Community

Old Orange County Courthouse: A Centennial History

Plano: An Illustrated Chronicle

The New Frontier:
A Contemporary History of Fort Worth & Tarrant County

The San Gabriel Valley: A 21st Century Portrait